Texas Folk Songs

Texas Folklore Society Publication XXIII

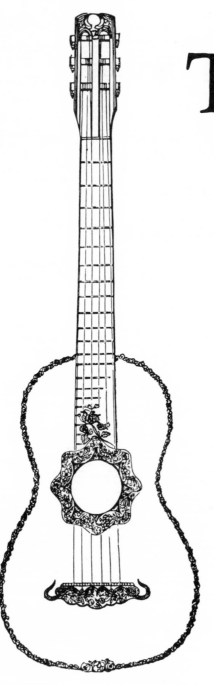

TEXAS

Musical transcriptions by
Jessie Ann Owens

FOLK SONGS

Second edition
Revised and enlarged by

WILLIAM A. OWENS

SMU PRESS · DALLAS

This volume was published with the support of the Texas Commission on the Arts and Humanities and the National Endowment for the Arts, a Federal Agency.

Library of Congress Cataloging in Publication Data

Owens, William A.   1905-   comp.
    Texas folk songs.
    (Publications of the Texas Folklore Society; no. 23)
Bibliography: p.
    Includes indexes.
    1. Folk-songs, American—Texas. I. Title.
II. Series: Texas Folklore Society. Publications; no. 23.
GR1.T4 no. 23 [M1629] 390'.08s [784.4'9764]
ISBN 0-87074-157-8   76-43005

CONTENTS

ANGLO-AMERICAN COMIC SONGS 103

SONGS AND GAMES FOR CHILDREN 134

PREFACE

THIS COLLECTION of songs began with those sung in my home in the Pin Hook community, Lamar County, Texas, when ballads and songs and spirituals seeped as easily as words into my memory. Then, when I was about fifteen, I began my own "ballit" book, in which I copied songs from relatives come to visit and from boys and girls at school who at dinner time sat under a brush arbor and passed around songs old and new. Songs were for enjoyment—for words and tunes and emotional release—from the popular war song "Till We Meet Again" to the old ballad of "The Jealous Lover." Indiscriminately the songs went into my "ballit" book.

Collecting did not become a serious project with me until my last year in college, when my interest in my own background came out in the open and I was urged to make a study of Texas play-party songs. I did, and the collection was published as *Swing and Turn: Texas Play-party Games* (1936). In the ten years following my graduation my collecting ranged from sporadic to intensive. At first the process was slow. I took down words from a singer and then went over the tune with him again and again, long enough to fix it in my mind. Then, with the help of friends better trained in music than I, I set the notes down.

My earliest collecting with sound equipment began at the end of 1937, when I bought a secondhand Vibromaster, a machine already antique. It embossed rather than cut on aluminum discs. The quality was not the best but the records were durable, so long as they were played with a fiber needle, preferably a cactus thorn. In the towns, where perhaps two homes out of three had a radio, the recordings were a novelty; in the country, where there might not be a radio within a radius of twenty miles or more, they were often regarded as miracles.

These recording trips began at Texas Agricultural and Mechanical College (now Texas A&M University), where I was teaching English, and where my students gave me leads to singers in both town and country, and extended farther and farther out as I managed travel time and expense money. Within a year I had recorded in Negro churches in the Brazos bottoms, Anglo-Saxon settlements in the Big Thicket, Cajun French communities in Southeast Texas and Louisiana, and Italian and Czech homes in Mumford and Rosebud. Folk music in the South had long been regarded as rural, "country," but the migration from country to town was well under way and the people took their folk songs and folk ways with them. To me, as a collector, an English ballad was an English ballad whether sung by a Dallas streetcar conductor or a sawmill hand in the piney woods. My pursuit of Anglo-Saxon ballads and songs took me to Oklahoma and then on into Missouri. Often the songs I found there were similar in words and tunes to those I had found in Texas, and I began to understand how songs had been carried along in westward migrations. By 1940 I had interviewed hundreds of potential singers and rejected many, recorded many. I had over three hundred recordings, and my knowledge of the people and their ways was clearer.

In 1941, through recommendations of J. Frank Dobie, Roy Bedichek, and Walter Prescott Webb, the president of the University of Texas authorized the formation of a library of recordings of Texas folk music and appointed me as researcher. Suddenly I found myself more adequately funded, provided with more sophisticated recording equipment, and directed to record anywhere in the state and among all ethnic groups. I had researched the territory east of the Colorado River reasonably well. Now I was able to spend time in the Mexican sections of San Antonio and other cities and to follow the Rio Grande from Brownsville to Del Rio, in search of ballads and songs that reflected the Mexican-American experience and the remnants of a Spanish heritage. I spent time with Germans in New Ulm, New Braunfels, and Fredericksburg, mostly listening to um-pah-pah bands. For cowboy songs, though they had already been widely collected and I found little that was new, I went as far south as the King Ranch and west to the New Mexico line.

In nine months I traveled thousands of miles and recorded the beginnings of a library that has become representative of Texas folk songs in all their wide variety. Then for several reasons, the impending World War II chief among them, I abruptly gave up collecting and within a few months enlisted as a private in the army. I gave it up, but not entirely. Even as a soldier I found time to record Peter Bell, a remarkable fiddler from Carrizo Springs, and to listen to the songs of Rod Drake.

My recording experience was relatively short in time, relatively wide-ranging in geography and peoples. This book, an extensive revision of the first edition of *Texas Folk Songs* (1950), is intended not as the whole but as a sampling of a rich experience in a richer land.

The songs of one singer, Rod Drake of the Drake settlement near Fred, show that richness. Over a dozen years I heard his singing and talked to him about his songs. Then in 1952 he taped forty-seven songs out of a wide knowledge of every kind in the Anglo-American tradition and a few in the Afro-American. He had lived his life in the isolation of the Big Thicket and had memorized every song he could find. The addition of his songs alone would make the issuance of this new edition imperative.

In two installments of my autobiography, *This Stubborn Soil* and *A Season of Weathering*, I included pieces of Anglo-American and Afro-American folk song and lore as they touched my life. In the third installment, in preparation at this writing—a volume devoted to experiences of Texas people as well as to my own—I will deal more extensively with those and add selections from the numerous songs I collected among the Cajun French, Mexican-American, and other ethnic groups coexisting in Texas.

I am deeply grateful to the singers—most of whom have passed on—whose contributions make up this book.

A grant from the Texas Commission on the Arts and Humanities and the National Endowment for the Arts helped make this edition possible. An appointment as writer in residence at Texas A&M University brought me back to the Texas scene and provided the time necessary for completing work on the volume. Again I am grateful.

WILLIAM A. OWENS

Nyack, New York
August, 1976

NOTES ON MUSICAL TRANSCRIPTIONS

FOLK SINGERS have no use for musical notation. They learn from other singers and they sing from memory. The transcriber, therefore, faces several problems when he tries to fit a notational system onto folk music.

Notation implies stability, a "right" way of singing a tune. Yet folk music is in a state of constant change. A singer may change the tune or the words from one day to the next, according to the vagaries of memory. The transcriptions should be understood as a description of one particular performance, not a prescription for how the song is to be sung.

Notation implies a system of ordering pitch and time. I have chosen Western staff notation because it usually fits the music well and it is familiar to most readers. I use many of its conventions, such as key signatures, time signatures, and barlines. It is important to understand that the concepts which underlie the conventions belong to the notation and not to the music.

I have transcribed most of the tunes in duple or triple meter, giving the quarter or dotted quarter note the beat. I have listed the metronome indication to show the tempo of the particular performance which was recorded. In some cases, because the original recording was unavailable, I have used the first edition of *Texas Folk Songs* or *Swing and Turn* as my source, checking the accuracy of the transcription with my father. For these songs I have not indicated a tempo.

Some songs, although they fit into a metric pattern, are not completely regular. For example, "The Boston Burglar" has many of the characteristics of 6/8 meter, yet the singer alters the lengths of some of the measures and varies the tempo over the course of the song. This sort of irregularity within an essentially regular metrical framework is particularly typical of Rod Drake's style. Instead of giving a tempo indication, I have made note of the flexibility in tempo and meter. I use the *fermata* (⌒) to show where the singer has lengthened a note.

xv

There are other songs whose rhythmic organization is not made clearer by trying to force them into a standard meter. Some derive their organization from verse accent ("The Little Sparrow," "Come All You Pretty Fair Maids," "Oh, Willie," and "Don't You See That Turtle Dove"); others from a steady pulse ("Little Mohea," "Brother Green," "William Hall" (a), "Late One Sunday Evening," and "The Grog Shop Door"). Finally, a few songs ("Come, All You Jolly Cowboys," "I Dreamed Last Night of My True Love," "The Three Little Babes," and "You Shall Be Free") have neither a regular metrical pattern nor a steady pulse. For their tempo I have listed "slow, without measure."

Sometimes singers ornament the melody, particularly in the slow, mournful songs. I used a grace note (♪) to show a brief, unmeasured embellishment either before or after the main note and the symbol to show a slide from one note to the next.

Occasionally in my notes on individual songs I have discussed musical form. I employ the convention of letting a capital letter (A, B, etc.) stand for a musical phrase, and a capital letter with a prime (A′, B′, etc.) stand for a slight variation of the phrase.

Most of the music in this collection was sung by a solo singer with no accompaniment. The decision whether to provide piano arrangements or even guitar chords is a difficult one. On the one hand, it is desirable that the edition meet the needs of its readers, most of whom are accustomed to songs furnished with some sort of accompaniment. On the other hand, it is clear that an edition which compromises authenticity serves no one. In the past, many popular collections of folk music, including the first edition of *Texas Folk Songs*, have included piano arrangements and/or guitar chords. The tunes were often versions made to fit the arrangements, surely a serious compromise.

The problem is that the tunes often are not tonal. Tonal accompaniments do not fit. My father says the same thing in a different way in *This Stubborn Soil*. He recalls that there were some tunes that his mother couldn't "second," couldn't provide with chordal accompaniment.

In practice the distinction between tunes that could be seconded and those that could not is often blurred. For example, several of the singers represented in this collection occasionally accompany themselves on the guitar. When they get to a section of the melody that doesn't fit the chord, they either omit the accompaniment for that particular section or ignore the dissonance.

In all cases where the singer provides accompaniment, whether or not the chords fit the tune well, I have included the chords in the transcription. In addition, for the benefit of the reader, I have provided chords for some of the tunes that seemed tonal, the tunes that one could "second." The reader should remember, however, that this is basically solo music.

I would like to conclude with a personal note. When I was not yet three years old, my father wrote in my copy of *Texas Folk Songs*: "For Jessie Ann, who will, I hope, have the spirit of Missouri Ann and the love her namesake had for these old songs. With deep love from Papa." My father could not have imagined when he signed my book that I would one day chose music as my profession or work with him on a new edition of the folk songs. My mother, as the peace keeper during the occasionally stormy collaboration between father and daughter, perhaps can attest to my spirit. I can attest to the second part of the inscription. Although I never knew the grandmother whose name I bear, I have heard her sing on tapes and discs and I have grown to love her music.

JESSIE ANN OWENS

Princeton, New Jersey
July, 1976

INTRODUCTION

ANGLO-SAXON, Anglo-American, Anglo-Texan: each of these terms is an extension of the preceding—one parent to the other, just as European is parent to all three, and to Spanish-American, Franco-American, any other European-American as well. Only the Afro-American is half-brother—half African, half European—a vigorous cultural offspring of an alliance regarded by many as unlikely, by some as misguided, even unfortunate. Judgments aside, Texas has become home to these various hybrids, and is the richer for it; but in the naming as well as in the minds of Anglo-Texans Anglo comes first, in rank as well as in number, and certainly in authenticity. Anything else, if regarded at all, is likely to be regarded as curiosity. Yet history reveals that folk music antedates all these namings, as well as the written history from which Anglo-Texans claim their heritage—a heritage that in time must embrace all. Folk music is common to all, regardless of origin. For all it records hopes, fears, joys, sorrows, at the same time providing history, music, and drama. It opens windows wide on all human experience.

Folk music is both stay-at-home and wanderer. It is stay-at-home wherever people have settled in one spot and maintained homogeneity generation after generation. In such circumstances—a Kentucky hollow, a Big Thicket community, for instance—it may be added to, taken from, polished, blemished, all in keeping with language, customs, beliefs of an isolated society, at the same time retaining elements identifiable with variants from other times, other places.

It is wanderer in the minds of those who through choice or compulsion leave the old home and journey to other lands, other shores. It is a wanderer in the mind of a wanderer. A song may be retained word for word in the mind of the carrier, or it may recount new knowledge, new experience as soon as new places, new happenings, new attitudes come into view. Such wanderings of Anglo-Saxon pioneers are clearly traceable as they crossed rivers and mountains and plains in their long journeys from the Atlantic to the Pacific and to the Mexican border. Similar wanderings are as clearly traceable earlier in the cognates of British ballads as they are preserved in Germany and Scandinavia. Less clearly traceable are the idioms in both language and music that are passed across geographical or political boundaries wherever people wander.

It is this wandering, gypsying, this ever changing, ever remaining the same that makes folk music useful in the study of a people. Or, as in the case of Texas, the study of ethnic groups living side by side, not homogeneous in spite of overlappings, a people only in terms of geographical and political necessity—a potential melting pot under which no group, especially the Anglo majority, ever felt like building a fire. The result is the perpetuation, consciously or unconsciously, of boundaries old as Europe, Africa, and America itself.

Though the cultural interchangings are numerous, the Anglo-Saxons, Anglo-Americans, Anglo-Texans remain predominant. Their folklore, perhaps more readily accessible, has been extensively collected and studied. From it, patterns of classification and criticism have emerged. It is, therefore, pragmatic if not in other ways defensible to focus on their folk music.

Texas Folk Songs

BRITISH POPULAR BALLADS

FOR THE PURPOSES of this book, a ballad is a song that tells a story. It is popular in that it persists widely among people in general; traditional in that it is handed down orally from generation to generation; British in that it had its origin in the British Isles or received the British stamp as it passed through.

Some of these ballads were in the minds of the earliest settlers, whether Anglicans in Virginia or Puritans in Massachusetts. A greater number were a part of the cultural baggage of English, Scots, Scotch-Irish, and Welsh who came to America in droves in the first half of the eighteenth century. These later settlers, instead of remaining on the Atlantic seaboard, rushed on through Pennsylvania, through the Shenandoah Valley, across the Allegheny Mountains, to settle in isolated valleys and hollows along westward-flowing rivers. In Britain, singers could have refreshed their memories of ballads from the printed pages of collections such as those of Sir Walter Scott. On the frontier a printed page of any kind was rare and the person who could read and write almost as rare.

People who could write sometimes set their songs down in "ballit" books and thus preserved versions reasonably faithful to those brought from Britain—versions with words but not tunes. Others simply sang words and tunes as they remembered them. As settlers fanned out over an ever widening frontier, the singers had to depend more and more on memory. The result was often a story fragmented, or filled out with words and stanzas from another ballad, until a ballad of death over unrequited love might be only slightly different from two or three others of death over unrequited love. Tunes were as frequently borrowed as words. Variants and variants of variants came into being as the new America moved farther and farther from the European prototype.

Much criticism has been written about the form as well as the substance of the popular ballad. In a collection like this all that seems necessary is to say that these

ballads found in Texas contain most of the conventions recognized by scholars: they
tell a story to a tune; they tell it objectively, tersely, with only the essential details
of character and setting; they present the action dramatically, often through dia-
logue; they tell it most often in a four-line stanza; they use such commonplace
phrases as "lilywhite hand" and "milk white steed"; they abound in conceits such
as that of the rose and briar that grow out of the graves of two dead lovers. More
often tragic, they sometimes become comic, as in "Our Goodman" and "The Wife
Wrapt in Wether's Skin."

One need not be well versed in the popular ballads as they appeared in Britain
to be able to recognize changes wrought by Americans, even Texans, on the frontier.
These changes occur in both language and attitudes. Most of the settlers came in
search of land and of political and religious freedom. As they came to new places
they added new place names. American names supplanted foreign names in balladry,
in instances like "I have a girl on the Arkansas line." Religious freedom included
the right to poke fun at religion. In Europe a man might be fined for not doffing
his hat to a priest; in Texas, singers could sing without penalty,

> Take her by the lilywhite hand
> And lead her like a pigeon;
> Make her dance to weevily wheat
> And scatter her religion.

Ballads brought by the earliest settlers took two hundred years or more to get
to Texas, and they came by various routes from starting points in Pennsylvania, Virginia, Carolina. As they traveled they separated when the people separated, came
together again when the people came together again. At times the changes they
underwent along the way were so great that kinship of one variant to another was
difficult to determine. Arguments arose over the "right way" to sing a song. There
are no rules for determining the right way to sing a ballad, as there are none for
calling a ballad "Texan." The ballads in this section did come to Texas, and Texas
singers have made their own adaptations. In this respect they can be called both
Texan and Anglo. They all appear in Francis James Child's work, *The English and
Scottish Popular Ballads*, a work that has set a high standard for authenticity of
origins.

ROSEMARY ONE TIME

This version of "The Elfin Knight" is the only one I found in Texas. Rod Drake
insisted on "rosemary one time" as the words. When I suggested "rosemary and
thyme" he rejected them. He had never heard of thyme.

Sung by Rod Drake, Silsbee, Texas, 1952.

As you go through that yonders town,
Rosemary one time,
Admire your address to that young lady
And ask her to be a true lovier of mine.

Tell her to make me a cambric shirt,
Rosemary one time,
Without a seam or a seamster's work,
And then she'll be a true lovier of mine.

Tell her to wash it at a dry well,
Rosemary one time,
Where rain never was and water never fell,
And then she'll be a true lovier of mine.

Tell her to dry it on a thorn,
Rosemary one time,
Where leaf never growed since Adam was borned,
And then she'll be a true lovier of mine.

Tell her when her work is all done,
Rosemary one time,
To let me know and I'll get my shirt,
And then she'll be a true lovier of mine.

As you go through that yonders town,
Rosemary one time,
Admire your address to that young man,
And ask him to be a true lovier of mine.

Tell him to plant me one acre of corn,
Rosemary one time,
Between the salt water and the sea shore,
And then he'll be a true lovier of mine.

Tell him to plough it with a thorn,
Rosemary one time,
Plant it all over with one grain of corn,
And then he'll be a true lovier of mine.

Tell him to reap it with a stirrup leather,
Rosemary one time,
Bind it all up in a peafowl feather,
And then he'll be a true lovier of mine.

Tell him to carry it to the mill,
Rosemary one time,
Every grain a bushel fill,
And then he'll be a true lovier of mine.

Tell him to thrash it against the wall,
Rosemary one time,
Whatever he does, don't let a grain fall,
And then he'll be a true lovier of mine.

Tell him when his work is all done,
Rosemary one time,
Come to this town and I'll give him his shirt,
And then he'll be a true lovier of mine.

PRETTY POLLY

Called "Lady Isabel and the Elf-Knight" in England and Scotland, "Pretty Polly" is the most widely known of all ballads, according to Francis James Child. Versions of it have been found in Germany, Poland, and Holland, as well as in the British Isles and America. In Texas, however, it is not nearly so well known as "Barbara Allen" and "Fair Ellender."

The version sung by Mrs. Ben Dryden is somewhat similar to an English version called "May Collin." The supernatural element has been lost, and the identity of the betrayer—an elf-knight, or false priest in some versions—is not revealed. The "six king's daughters" of the English versions have become in Texas "six of the old Virginny girls." In some renditions Pretty Polly confides her story to her "pretty parrot" and begs him not to tell her parents.

a. Sung by Rod Drake, Silsbee, Texas, 1952. The third line, which does not occur in the first two verses, is included here with the text from the third verse.

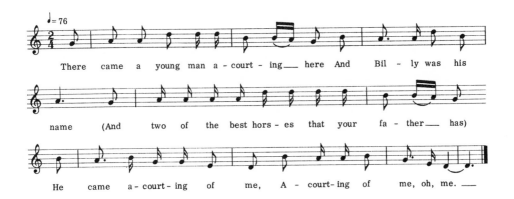

There came a young man a-courting here
And Billy was his name;
[*Third line not sung.*]
He came a-courting of me,
A-courting of me, oh, me.

He courted me up, he courted me down,
I had no wings to fly away;
[*Third line not sung.*]
No tongue to tell him no, no, no,
No tongue to tell him no.

"Go rob your mother of her fee,
Your father of his gold,
And two of the best horses that your father has,
Likewise he thirty and three, three, three,
Likewise he thirty and three."

She robbed her mother of her fee,
Her father of his gold,
And two of the best horses that her father had,
Likewise he thirty and three, three, three,
Likewise he thirty and three.

He mounted on a double black,
And she on a dapple gray,
And they rode till they came to the deep water side,
In the length of a long summer day, day, day,
In the length of a long summer day.

"Oh, light you down, Pretty Polly,
Oh, light you down," says he,
"Six king's daughters all drownded here,
And the seventh you will be, be, be,
And the seventh you will be."

She turned herself all around and about
To view the green leaves on the tree;
She takened him by his slender waist
And she plunged him into the sea, sea, sea,
And she plunged him into the sea.

"Oh, help me out, Pretty Polly,
Oh, help me out," says he,
"And to New England we will go
And married we will be, be, be,
And married we will be."

"Swim there, swim there, you false young man,
Swim there, swim there," says she,
"Oh, ain't it a pity such costly wear
Will be rotting in the old salt sea, sea, sea,
Will be rotting in the old salt sea."

She mounted on the double black,
And she led the dapple gray,
And she rode till she come to her own father's door
Two hours before it was day, day, day,
Two hours before it was day.

"Crow there, crow there, you pretty crowing fowl,
Crow there, crow there," says she,
"Your wings shall be mounted with shining gold,
And your comb with the ivory so gay, gay, gay,
And your comb with the ivory so gay."

b. Sung by Mrs. Ben Dryden, Fred, Texas, 1941. There is considerable rhythmic flexibility.

"Go bring me some of your fa - ther's gold And bring me your mo-ther's fee.

Oh, come, oh,— come my— Pret-ty Pol - ly And go a-long with me.

"Go bring me some of your father's gold
And bring me your mother's fee.
Oh, come, oh, come my Pretty Polly
And go along with me.

"I'll take you down by the seashore side,
And there I'll marry thee."
She mounted on her milk white horse
And to some dark she rode.

She rode till she came to the salt water sea,
Where there's none that she could see;
She rode till she came to the salt water sea,
Where there's no one that she could see.

"Get down, get down, my Pretty Polly,
And rein your horse to a tree;
For I have killed six of the old Virginny girls
And the seventh one you shall be.

"Get down, get down, my Pretty Polly,
And rein your horse to a tree;
Pull off them rings, pull off them pearls,
And lay them on my knee;

"For they are too rich and they are too gay
For to lie in the salt water sea;
For they are too rich and they are too gay
For to lie in the salt water sea."

"Oh, turn your back and place your eyes
Along the' juniper tree;
Oh, turn your back and place your eyes
Along the juniper tree."

She pushed him into the salt water sea,
Where there's no one that he could see;
She pushed him into the salt water sea,
Where there's no one that he could see.

"Reach down your hand, Pretty Polly, I pray,
Reach down your hand to me;
I'll carry you back to your own father's house
Two long hours 'fore it came day."

"Oh, hush, oh, hush, you grand rascal,
And say no more to me,
For it's I shall go to my old father's house
Two long hours 'fore it came day."

"Where have you been, my Pretty Polly,
Where have you been I pray?
Where have you been, my Pretty Polly,
This long summer day."

"Oh, hush, oh, hush, my pretty parent,
And tell no tales on me,
For your house shall be lined with the finest of gold,
And your doors with ivory.

"For I have been to the salt water sea,
Where there's no one that I can see;
For that is six of the old Virginny girls
And the seventh one he shall be."

BILLY BOY

In Lamar County, Texas, "Billy Boy" was sung as a "funny" song and as a riddle. The comic element is in the parody of "Lord Randall," though the latter apparently was never sung in that area. The stanzas here are only samples of the many improvisations. The riddle was in the last stanza and her age varied as the singers tried to think up more difficult addition and multiplication.

Sung by William A. Owens.

"Oh, where have you been, Billy Boy, Billy Boy?
Oh, where have you been, charming Billy?"
"I have been to seek a wife, she's the darling of my life,
She's a young thing and cannot leave her mother."

"Can she bake a cherry pie, Billy Boy, Billy Boy?
Can she bake a cherry pie, charming Billy?"
"She can bake a cherry pie quicker'n a gnat can wink his eye,
She's a young thing and cannot leave her mother."

"Can she make a feather bed, Billy Boy, Billy Boy?
Can she make a feather bed, charming Billy?"
"She can make a feather bed with the feet up at the head,
She's a young thing and cannot leave her mother."

"Did she ask you to come in, Billy Boy, Billy Boy?
Did she ask you to come in, charming Billy?"
"Yes, she asked me to come in, she had grease on her chin,
She's a young thing and cannot leave her mother."

"How old is she, Billy Boy, Billy Boy?
How old is she, charming Billy?"
"Twice six, twice seven, forty-nine and eleven,
She's a young thing and cannot leave her mother."

HOW COME THAT BLOOD ON YOUR SHIRT SLEEVE

This ballad came to me first as a fragment from Mrs. C. H. Burke of Silsbee.
Mr. and Mrs. Irvin Thompson had arranged for me to record at their home. When
I had the recording machine set up they sent for Mrs. Burke, only to be told that
she had gone to the woods to pray, as she did every morning. After a while she came
to the house and though it was against her religion, sang a dozen or so songs, among
them "The Boston Burglar" and "Little Mohea." She finally told me that she knew
one more song, but that it was too old for me to want. She sang enough of it, however, for me to recognize it as "Edward."

It was several years before I located a complete version of the song. This time
the singer was Mrs. Ben Dryden of the Sandy Creek settlement. Since then I have
found several more versions, but none as full as Mrs. Dryden's. I heard all of these
in Southeast Texas and was unable to find the song elsewhere in the state. Collectors
from other parts of the United States have reported it only a few times.

The version printed by Bishop Thomas Percy (*Reliques of English Poetry*;
3 vols., 1765) is a story of patricide, with a suggestion of incest as the motive. In
the versions I have found the crime in invariably fratricide, and there is no hint of
incest. The murder always grows out of an argument over cutting down a juniper
tree.

In one Texas version the answer to the opening question is, "It is the blood of
my guinea gew hawk," and the song is called "The Guinea Gew Hawk." It apparently has no relation to "The Gay Goshawk."

a. Sung by Mrs. C. H. Burke, Silsbee, Texas, 1938.

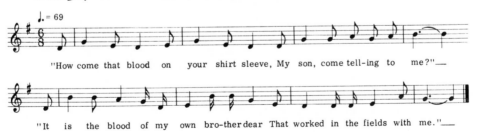

"How come that blood on your shirt sleeve, My son, come tell-ing to me?"—

"It is the blood of my own bro-ther dear That worked in the fields with me."—

"How come that blood on your shirt sleeve,
My son, come telling to me?"
"It is the blood of my own brother dear
That worked in the fields with me."

"What did you kill him for, my son,
My son, come telling to me?"
"I killed him for cutting yonders bush
That might have made a tree."

"What will you do when your father comes home,
My son, come telling to me?"
"I'll set my foot on yonder ship
And sail across the sea."

"What will you do with your children three,
My son, come telling to me?"
"I'll leave them here with my own mother dear
To keep her company."

"What will you do with your pretty little wife,
My son, come telling to me?"
"I'll take her by her lily-white hand
To sail along with me."

"When you coming back to see your children three,
My son, come telling to me?"
"Whene'er the sun sets on yonders green hill,
Which you know will never be."

b. Sung by Mrs. Ben Dryden, Fred, Texas, 1941.

This song presents several difficulties for transcription of the pitch. The singer omits the first line, starting somewhat uncertainly with the second. During the course of the first stanza she moves through several keys. By the second and third stanzas the pitch has stabilized to the version given in the transcription.

["How come that blood on your shirt sleeve,]
My son, come tell to me?
How come that blood on your shirt sleeve,
My son, come tell to me?"
"It is the blood of the old grey mare
That pulled the plow for me;
It is the blood of the old grey mare
That pulled the plow for me."

"That blood's too red for that,
My son, come tell to me,
How come that blood on your shirt sleeve,
My son, come tell to me?"
"It is the blood of the old grey hound
That chased the deer for me;
It is the blood of the old grey hound
That chased the deer for me."

"That blood's too red for that,
My son, come tell to me,
How come that blood on your shirt sleeve,
My son, come tell to me?"
"It is the blood of the old grey goose
That flew by the side of me;
It is the blood of the old grey goose
That flew by the side of me."

"That blood's too red for that,
My son, come tell to me,
How come that blood on your shirt sleeve,
My son, come tell to me?"
It is the blood of my own dear brother
That plowed by the side of me;
It is the blood of my own dear brother
That plowed by the side of me."

"What did you and your brother fall out about,
My son, come tell to me?"
[*Lines 3 and 4 missing.*]
"We fell out about that little Juniper tree
That grows under yander tree."

"What you gonna do when your father comes home,
My son, come tell to me?"
[*Lines 3 and 4 missing.*]
"I'll set my foot in a sailing boat
And sail across the sea."

"What you gonna do with your pretty little wife,
My son, come tell to me?"

[*Lines 3 and 4 missing.*]
"I'll set her foot by the side of my side,
Sail across the sea."

"What you gonna do with your pretty little children,
My son, come tell to me?"
[*Lines 3 and 4 missing.*]
"I'll leave them here in youry care
Till I return to thee."

"When you coming back
My son, come tell to me?"
[*Lines 3 and 4 missing.*]
"I'm coming back when the sun goes east and west
And that shall never be."

THREE BLACK CROWS

This song was first brought to my attention by Samuel Lee Asbury of College Station, himself a collector of ballads and religious folk songs. He said he had learned it when he was a boy in the Carolinas about 1880. In his version the song had been changed from the tragedy of the slain knight and his wife heavy with child to a comic song for entertaining and frightening children. In this respect, it is nearer the Scottish version, "The Twa Corbies," than it is the English, "The Three Ravens." When singing it, "Doc" Asbury kept his voice fairly low through the stanza and then screamed "Caw, caw, caw" in an ear-splitting shriek.

Later I found several persons in the Big Thicket area who knew this song, but their versions were not significantly different, and none of them had the dramatic interest of "The Three Ravens." All the tunes I heard for this song in Texas were more or less similar to that of "When Johnny Comes Marching Home."

An interesting variant of the song has been found among Negro singers in Texas:

Three little crows sat on a limb,
(Johnny mee-kee-mee-coy)
One little crow said to de othah,
(Johnny mee-kee-mee-coy)
"What'll we have to eat, little brothah?"
(Johnny mee-kee-mee-coy)
And dey flop dere wings an' cried,
"Johnny mee-kee-mee-coy."

Sung by Samuel Lee Asbury, College Station, Texas, 1938.

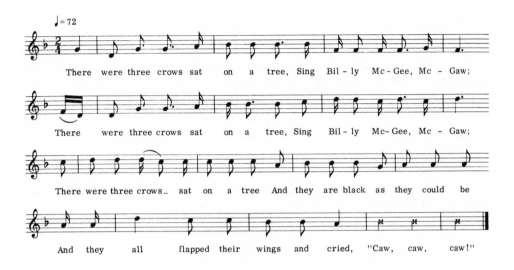

There were three crows sat on a tree, Sing Bil - ly Mc - Gee, Mc - Gaw;

There were three crows sat on a tree, Sing Bil - ly Mc - Gee, Mc - Gaw;

There were three crows_ sat on a tree And they are black as they could be

And they all flapped their wings and cried, "Caw, caw, caw!"

There were three crows sat on a tree,
Sing Billy McGee, McGaw;
There were three crows sat on a tree,
Sing Billy McGee, McGaw;
There were three crows sat on a tree
And they were black as they could be
And they all flapped their wings and cried, "Caw, caw, caw!"

Says one old crow unto his mate,
Sing Billy McGee, McGaw;
Says one old crow unto his mate,
Sing Billy McGee, McGaw;
Says one old crow unto his mate,
Oh, what shall we do for something to eat?
And they all flapped their wings and cried, "Caw, caw, caw!"

There lies a horse on yonders plain,
Oh, Billy McGee, McGaw;
There lies a horse on yonders plain,
Oh, Billy McGee, McGaw;
There lies a horse on yonders plain,
Who's by some cruel butcher slain;
And they all flopped their wings and cried, "Caw, caw, caw!"

We'll perch ourselves on his backbone,
Oh, Billy McGee, McGaw;
We'll perch ourselves on his backbone,
Oh, Billy McGee, McGaw;
We'll perch ourselves on his backbone,
And eat his eyeballs one by one;
And they all flopped their wings and cried, "Caw, caw, caw!"

LOVING HENRY

Scott's Lord Hunting has become Loving Henry and his Clyde Water the Arkansas line, in a change of class and location, but the story and the ballad remains essentially the same. Loving Henry comes to see Lady Margaret, his mistress, to tell her that he has found another love. Lady Margaret entices him with kisses, and then stabs him with a penknife. In some versions they discover that they love each other, but too late. In this one he dies and "some," not identified but apparently Lady Margaret's friends, throw his body into the water, with her exulting words that the "girl on the Arkansas line" will think him a long time coming home.

This song came with my grandmother's family in their journey by oxcart from Arkansas. No doubt the addition of "the Arkansas line" was made after they arrived in Texas.

Sung by Mrs. Bernice Kitchens, Blossom, Texas, 1938.

"Come in, come in, lov-ing Hen-ry," she said, "And stay all night with me,

For it's been a-bout three lone-some_ months Since I spoke one word with thee."

"Come in, come in, loving Henry," she said,
"And stay all night with me,
For it's been about three lonesome months
Since I spoke one word with thee."

"I can't come in, Lady Margaret," he said,
"And stay all night with thee,
For the girl that I've left on the Arkansas line
Thinks I'm a long time coming home."

As they stood out by the fence
A-taking kisses so sweet,
Lady Margaret had open knife within her hand
And she pierced him keen and deep.

"Go live, go live, loving Henry," she said,
"Go live for ever more,
For it's all those doctors we have within our town
Shall be brought here for your cure."

"How can I live, Lady Margaret," he said,
"How can I live any more

When my own heart's blood comes dribbling down
And my breath is growing slow?"

Some took him by his lily-white hand,
Some took him by his feet,
And they carried him down to the broad water's edge
And plunged him into the deep.

"Lie there, lie there, loving Henry," she said,
"Lie there for ever more,
For the girl that you left on the Arkansas line
Thinks you're a long time coming home."

FAIR ELLENDER

"Fair Ellender" has a long history. First published as a broadside during the reign of Charles II, it was included in Percy's *Reliques* in 1765. It is still widely sung in the United States, and was traditional in my father's family—who may have brought it along from Tennessee, where similar versions have been found by Campbell and Sharp, or picked it up in Indiana, from which Brewster reports versions much like the one sung by my father. It has at times been confused with a ballad called "Fair Margaret and Sweet William." I have not found a version of the latter in Texas.

Sung by May Kennedy McCord, Springfield, Missouri, 1939.

Variant ending for verses in which the fourth line is repeated:

Lord Thomas he was a gay gentleman,
The lord of many a belle,
Fair Ellender was a fair young girl,
Lord Thomas he loved her well,
Lord Thomas he loved her well.

"Oh, father, oh, mother, come riddle to me,
I ask you both as one,
Oh, must I marry Fair Ellender,
Or bring the brown girl home?
Or bring the brown girl home?"

"The brown girl she has houses and lands,
Fair Ellender she has none,
Oh, son, we advise you as a great blessing
To bring the brown girl home,
To bring the brown girl home."

He dressed himself in satin robes,
His waiters all dressed in green,
And every town he rode through
They took him to be some king,
They took him to be some king.

He rode till he came to Fair Ellender's door,
He tingled at the ring,
And none so ready as she herself
To rise and bid him come in,
To rise and bid him come in.

"What news, what news, Lord Thomas," she cried,
"What news do you bring to me?"
"I've come to bid you to my wedding,
The brown girl my bride to be,
The brown girl my bride to be."

"Sad news, sad news, Lord Thomas," she cried,
"Sad news do you bring to me,
For I had hoped to be your bride
And you bridegroom to me,
And you bridegroom to me."

"Oh, father, oh, mother, come riddle to me,
I ask you both as one,
Oh, must I go to Lord Thomas' wedding
Or tarry with you at home?
Or tarry with you at home?

"For many there be who be my friends,
And many who be my foes,
But I will risk my fortune and life

And to Lord Thomas' wedding I'll go,
And to Lord Thomas' wedding I'll go."

She dressed herself in satin white,
Her ladies all dressed in green,
And every town that they rode through
They took her to be some queen,
They took her to be some queen.

She rode till she came to Lord Thomas' hall,
She tingled at the ring,
And none so ready as he himself
To rise and bid her come in,
To rise and bid her come in.

He took her by the lily-white hand,
He led her down the hall,
And seated her at the table's head
Among the ladies all,
Among the ladies all.

"Is this your bride, Lord Thomas?" she cried,
"She is a most wonderful brown,
When you could have had the fairest lady
That ever the sun shone on,
That ever the sun shone on."

"Throw none of your slurs," Lord Thomas he cried,
"Throw none of your slurs at me,
For I love the tip of your finger more
Than the brown girl's whole body,
Than the brown girl's whole body."

The brown girl had a little penknife
With blade both keen and sharp;
Between the short ribs and the long
She pierced Fair Ellender's heart,
She pierced Fair Ellender's heart.

"Oh, what is the matter, Fair Ellen?" he cried,
"What makes you look so pale?
You used to have as rosy cheeks
As anyone in our dale,
As anyone in our dale."

"Oh, are you blind, Lord Thomas?" she cried,
"Or is it you cannot see
That I can feel my whole heart's blood
Come trickling to my knee?
Come trickling to my knee?"

He took the brown girl by the hand,
He led her down the hall,
And with his sword cut off her head
And kicked it against the wall,
And kicked it against the wall.

He pointed the handle to the sun,
The blade unto his breast,
Saying, "Here's the death of two fond lovers,
God send our souls to rest,
God send our souls to rest.

"Go dig my grave 'neath yonder green tree,
Go dig it both wide and deep,
And place Fair Ellender in my arms
And the brown girl at my feet;
And the brown girl at my feet."

WHO WILL SHOE YOUR PRETTY LITTLE FOOT

The two stanzas printed here, from a British ballad which has existed in manuscript since the first part of the eighteenth century, are widely known in Texas; but I have been unable to find more than a fragment of the ballad. That is strange, since the whole ballad story is an easy one to remember. Annie of Roch Royal takes her young son in her arms and goes to search for his father, Love Gregory. When she comes to his door, his mother answers and tells her that Love Gregory has gone over the sea. Annie goes on in her quest. Love Gregory awakes and tells his mother he dreamed that Annie had been at the door. He starts out in search of her and finds her and her son drowned and floating in the foam. Then he dies of grief.

I have heard these two stanzas sung to at least a dozen different tunes in Texas. The first presented here is more often called "The Green Valley Waltz" and is a favorite with fiddle bands.

a. Sung by a group in Odessa, Texas, 1941.

Oh, who will shoe your pret-ty lit-tle foot, And who will glove your hand,___

And___ who will kiss your sweet___ ro-sy lips, When you come from that far-off land?___

Oh, who will shoe your pretty little foot,
And who will glove your hand,
And who will kiss your sweet rosy lips,
When you come from that far-off land?

My father will shoe my pretty little foot,
My mother will glove my hand,
My sweetheart will kiss my sweet rosy lips,
When you're in some far-off land.

b. Sung by Rod Drake, Silsbee, Texas, 1952.
Rhythmic organization is based on the structure of the poetic line.

Don't you see ____ that tur-tle dove? I see it in yon-ders pine,
A-mourn-ing for ____ its own true _ love, Just like ____ I mourn for mine.

Don't you see that turtle dove?
I see it in yonders pine,
A-mourning for its own true love,
Just like I mourn for mine.

Oh, who will glove your hands, my love,
And who will shoe your feet,
And who will kiss your rosy lips
While I'm in a foreign land?

My father will shoe my feet, my love,
My mother will glove my hand,
And you can kiss my rosy lips
When you return again.

Ten thousand miles will be my love
Doing Scotland's pain,
And if I go ten thousand more
I'm coming back again.

THE THREE LITTLE BABES

Sir Walter Scott, in his *Minstrelsy of the Scottish Border,* called this song "The Wife of Usher's Well." I heard it first in Texas when Mrs. Ben Dryden of the Sandy Creek settlement near Fred sang it for me in June, 1941. After that I heard it several times, always in the vicinity of the Big Thicket. Mrs. Dryden, who had lived more than fifty years in Sandy Creek, learned the song when she was a child from people who came from the Tennessee mountains. After she had recorded the song for me, I asked her to sing "The Wife of Usher's Well." "I ain't never heard of that song," she replied.

This song, apparently of Scottish origin, was popular in Scotland and England and has been widely reported in the United States. The version printed here is somewhat garbled. The story in general is of a mother who sent her three sons away to learn their Bible Book. While they were away they all were drowned. The mother, in her great grief, begged them to return to her. They did come at night. She set the table for them with bread and wine, but they had to refuse her because the Savior had divine food for them. They also refused to lie in the bed she had made for them, though she spread it with a "golden wand." Then when the dawn came, they had to go away. An English version explains their reason for going more effectively:

> The cock doth craw, the day doth daw,
> The channerin worm doth chide;
> Gin we be mist out o our place,
> A sair pain we maun abide.

In a version sung for me by Rod Drake of the Drake settlement near Silsbee the mother

> . . . sent her three little babes to the North Country
> To learn their grammaree.

Grammaree is an old Scotch word meaning magic. That meaning has been lost to East Texans and they associate the word in some way with schoolbooks. In another version from the same area the babes are sent to North Carolina—another demonstration of how local place names creep into ballads.

Sung by Mrs. Ben Dryden, Fred, Texas, 1941.

Slow, without measure

Once there was   a poor___ wi - dow woman, The   mo - ther of ___ three lit - tle babes;

She sent her three lit - tle babes a - way   To learn__ their___ Bi - ble Book.

> Once there was a poor widow woman,
> The mother of three little babes;
> She sent her three little babes away
> To learn their Bible Book.
>
> They had not gone but about three weeks,
> I'm sure it was not four
> Till there came a flood and washed her three little babes away
> And she began to weep and mourn,
>
> Saying, "Come to me, my three little babes,
> Tonight or in the morning soon."
> Her three little babes came wandering down
> Into their mother's arms.
>
> Saying, "We can't come to you, dear mother,
> But you can come to us,

For yander stands our dear Savior
And to Him we must obey."

She fixed them a table
All with bread and wine,
Saying, "Come and eat and drink with me,
Come on, my three little babes."

Up riz up the oldest one,
Saying, "We cain't eat your bread, dear mother,
Nor neither drink your wine;

"For yander stands our dear Savior,
And to Him we must obey."
She fixed them a bed all in the back room,
She fixed it with all clean sheets.

And on the top she spread a golden wand
To make them all sleep warm;
And on the top she spread a golden wand
To make them all sleep warm.

Up riz up the oldest one,
Early in the morning soon,
Saying, "Yander stands our dear Savior,
And to Him we must obey."

BARBARA ALLEN

If I were asked to name the ballad most deeply ingrained in the heart and thinking of the American folk, "Barbara Allen" would be my choice. I have heard it up and down the country against backgrounds ranging from expensive nightclubs to sharecroppers' shacks. Not once have I heard it burlesqued; the emotion it inspires is apparently too deep for that.

In the fall of 1938 a friend took me to see Bob Brown, an old-timer who lived on the road between Kountze and Sour Lake at the edge of the Big Thicket. In answer to our request for songs, he replied that he knew "Sweet William." Needing little urging, he leaned against a picket fence and sang this version of "Barbara Allen." When he came to the line, "Young man, I think you're dying," tears filled his eyes and he brushed at his wrinkled cheek with the back of his hand. He showed no embarrassment, nor offered any apology for his sentiment.

a. Sung by May Kennedy McCord, Springfield, Missouri, 1939. The chords are from the singer's guitar accompaniment.

In Scarlet town where I was born
There was a fair maid dwelling,
Made every youth cry, "Way-la-way,
Oh, here comes Barbara Allen."

'Twas in the merry month of May,
The green buds were a-swelling,
Sweet William on his deathbed lay
For the love of Barbara Allen.

They sent a servant to the town
Where Barbara was a-dwelling,
Saying, "Rise, oh, rise you up and go
If your name be Barbara Allen."

So slowly, slowly she rose up,
And slowly she came nigh him,
And these the words she said to him
Was, "Young man, I think you're dying."

"Oh, yes, I'm sick and very sick,
And death is on me dwelling,
And one sweet kiss would comfort me
From the lips of Barbara Allen."

"Oh, yes, you're sick and very sick,
And death is on you dwelling,
But one sweet kiss you never will have
From the lips of Barbara Allen.

"Oh, don't you remember on a wedding night
When we were at the tavern,
You drank a health to the ladies round,
But you slighted Barbara Allen?"

"Oh, yes, I remember on a wedding night
When we were at the tavern,
I drank a health to the ladies round,
But my heart was Barbara Allen's."

He turned his face to the pale cold wall,
And death was on him dwelling;
"Farewell, farewell to all false maids,
And woe to Barbara Allen."

When she was walking in the field
She heard the death bell knelling,
And every toll, it seemed to say,
"Hard-hearted Barbara Allen."

She looked to the east, she looked to the west,
And she saw the cold corpse coming.
"Lay down, lay down that cold, cold corpse
That I may gaze upon him."

The more she looked, the more she mourned
Till she fell to the ground a-crying,
Saying, "Pick me up and carry me home,
For I am now a-dying.

"Oh, mother, mother, go make my shroud,
Go make it long and narrow;
Sweet William died for me today,
I'll die for him tomorrow.

"Oh, father, father, go dig my grave,
Go dig it long and narrow;
Sweet William died for me for love,
I'll die for him for sorrow."

They buried her in the lone church yard,
Sweet William lay a-nigh her,
And out of his grave grew a red, red rose,
And out of hers grew a briar.

They climbed, they climbed to the tall church top,
Till they could go no higher,
And there they tied in a true lover's knot,
The rose wrapped around the briar.

b. Sung by Mrs. I. L. Stowe, Silsbee, Texas, 1938.

It was the mer - ry month of June When the red rose was bloom-ing, —

Sweet Wil - liam rode from a north coun - try, Fell in love with Bar - bry Al - len. —

It was the merry month of June
When the red rose was blooming,
Sweet William rode from a north country,
Fell in love with Barbry Allen.

He sent his servant down to town
Where Miss Barbry was dwelling.
"My master said tell please come down
If you please, Miss Barbry Allen."

Slowly, slowly she got up
And slowly she went to him,
And thus'n she said unto him,
"Young man, I think you're dying."

He turned his pale face to the wall,
She turned her face upon him.
He said, "Kind friends, stand around my bed,
Remember Barbry Allen."

As she was walking up and down the street
She saw his cold corpse coming,
And at the corner of every street
Saying, "Woe to Barbry Allen."

THE HANGMAN'S ROPE

This ballad, recorded for me by Mrs. I. L. Stowe of Silsbee, is widely sung in
Southeast Texas, but is less well known in other parts of the state. The dozen or
so versions I have heard vary surprisingly little, perhaps because of the simplicity
of words and story, and the incremental repetition.

In most versions, English and American, a girl is faced with hanging on the
gallows if her fine is not paid. In the English version the appeal is to the judge
or justice of the peace rather than to the executioner. In some of these she is to be
hanged for stealing a golden ball or a comb. In the ones I have heard in Texas
details of her crime are omitted. In a few versions, particularly those sung by southern Negroes, a youth instead of a maid is freed from the gallows.

Two versions I have heard in Negro dialect begin "Slack-a-man, slack-a-man,
lack on yo' line" and "Hangerman, hangerman, slack yo' rope."

Sung by Mrs. I. L. Stowe, Silsbee, Texas, 1938.

"Oh, hang-man, hang-man, slack your rope, Oh, slack it for a while; ___
I think I see my own dear fa-ther Come rid-ing ma-ny a mile." ___

"Oh, hangman, hangman, slack your rope,
Oh, slack it for a while;
I think I see my own dear father
Come riding many a mile."

"Oh, father, did you bring my gold,
Or did you pay my fee,
Or did you come to see me hanged
To yonders willow tree?"

"Oh, no, I did not bring your gold,
And did not pay your fee;
I come to see you hang today
To yonders willow tree."

[*The same formula is repeated for mother, sister, brother.*]

"Oh, hangman, hangman, slack your rope,
Oh, slack it for a while;
I think I see my own true love
Come riding many a mile.

"Oh, true love, did you bring my gold,
Or did you pay my fee,
Or did you come to see me hanged
To yonders willow tree?"

"Oh, yes, I brought your gold, my dear,
And also paid your fee;
I did not come to see you hanged
To yonders willow tree."

THE FOUR MARYS

The two stanzas and refrain presented here are from the last part of a long ballad called "Mary Hamilton," which has been reported from Virginia and Maine but is not well known in the United States. When Mary Stuart was sent to France in 1548 she was accompanied by Mary Fleming, Mary Livingston, Mary Seton, and Mary Beaton. They all remained with her during her residence in France and returned to Scotland with her in 1561. The ballad is apparently the story of one of the four Marys, though the names have been considerably altered.

In the complete version Mary Hamilton is with child by the "highest Stewart of all." The child is born and she drowns it. When she is found out, she is sentenced to death. The words in this fragment are spoken by her as she is mounting the stairs to the gallows.

I first heard these stanzas from the Bohler family, who made their living by fishing from a houseboat on the Neches River, at that time tied up near a bridge east of Silsbee.

Sung by an unknown hitchhiker in East Texas, 1941.

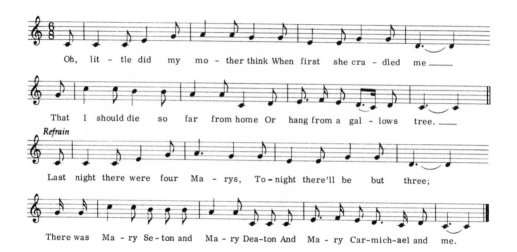

Oh, little did my mother think
When first she cradled me
That I should die so far from home
Or hang from a gallows tree.

Refrain:
> Last night there were four Marys,
> Tonight there'll be but three;
> There was Mary Seton and Mary Deaton
> And Mary Carmichael and me.

They'll tie a napkin round my eyes,
They'll not let me see the deed,
And they'll never let on to my father and mother
But what I have gone o'er the sea.
    (*Refrain*)

GYPSY DAVY

In the traditional Scottish ballad "The Gypsy Laddie," the gypsies sing outside the castle gate until the lady comes down to hear them. Then they "coost the glamer o'er her" and she goes away with Johnny Faa, the gypsy laddie. Johnny Faa and seven other gypsies were executed in 1624. The Texas versions, of which there are several, fail to mention Johnny Faa, and Gypsy Davy is alone in practicing his charms.

What I consider the most interesting American version of this ballad was printed by DeMarsan as a broadside about 1860. The dialect may be genuinely Negro, but more likely it is the work of a white minstrel singer.

> There was a lord, a high born lord,
> Who courted a high born lady;
> She lived in a palace all so grand,
> Till she met with the Gipsey Davy.
>
> *Refrain:*
>> Elopements now are all the go,
>> They set the darkies crazy;
>> Take warning all, both great and small,
>> And beware of the Gipsey Davy.
>
> This lord he was a fine young man,
> And he set this lady crazy,
> So she packed up her duds and away she ran
> Along with the Gipsey Davy.
>> (*Refrain*)
>
> Her parents raved and tore their hair,
> When they come for to miss that ere baby,
> And then to think of that sweet born baby,
> None knew but the Gipsey Davy.
>> (*Refrain*)
>
> Oh, how could she leave her house and lands,
> Oh, how could she leave her baby,
> Oh, how could she leave her own wedded hand
> To run off with the Gipsey Davy!
>> (*Refrain*)
>
> Last night she laid in a dear feather bed,
> And in her arms her baby;
> Tonight she'll lay on the cold, cold ground,
> In the arms of Gipsey Davy.
>> (*Refrain*)

Sung by May Kennedy McCord, Springfield, Missouri, 1939. The chords are from the singer's guitar accompaniment.

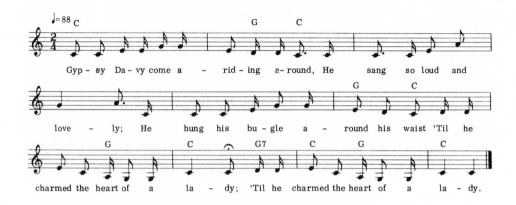

Gypsy Davy come a-riding around,
He sang so loud and lovely;
He hung his bugle around his waist
'Til he charmed the heart of a lady;
'Til he charmed the heart of a lady.

"Come go with me, my pretty fine miss,
Come go with me, my honey;
Come go with me, my pretty fine miss,
You shall never want for money;
You shall never want for money."

She put on her fine new Sunday shoes
All made of Spanish leather;
He put on his old cork boots,
And they both rode off together;
And they both rode off together.

Her husband he came home that night
Inquiring for his lady;
He was informed by a pretty fair maid,
"She's gone with the Gypsy Davy;
She's gone with the Gypsy Davy."

"Go saddle me up my blondale horse
And hand me down my flagon;
I'll ride to the east and I'll ride to the west
'Til I overtake my lady;
'Til I overtake my lady."

He rode till he came to the banks of the stream,
The sea was dark and muddy;
The tears came a-rolling down his cheeks,
For there he spied his honey;
For there he spied his honey.

"Will you forsake your home," he cried,
"Will you forsake your baby?
Will you forsake your husband, too,
To go with the Gypsy Davy;
To go with the Gypsy Davy?"

"Yes, I'll forsake my home," she cried,
"And I'll forsake my baby,
And I'll forsake my husband, too,
To go with the Gypsy Davy;
To go with the Gypsy Davy."

"Last night you slept on a fair white bed
Between me and your baby;
Tonight you're a-sleepin' on the cold, cold ground,
A-sleeping with the Gypsy Davy;
A-sleeping with the Gypsy Davy."

THE HOUSE CARPENTER

When as an undergraduate in college I came across a copy of "The Daemon Lover" as written by Sir Walter Scott, the song seemed so familiar that I asked my mother about it. She sang "The House Carpenter" for me and I remembered then that she had often sung it when I was a child. It is essentially the same song that Scott published in 1812 except that the lover has lost the name "James Harris" and is no longer a demon, his demonic nature having no doubt been rationalized out as the superstition of congress between men and demons became fainter. In the last stanza, however, the "dark and dreary eye" may still possibly refer to a person with supernatural qualities. In the British versions the lovers both drown when their ship goes down in a storm. The version presented here is the only one I know in which the woman commits suicide.

This ballad is widely known in the United States. About 1860 it appeared on the streets of New York as a penny song sheet.

Sung by Mrs. Jessie Ann Chennault Smith, Blossom, Texas, 1938.

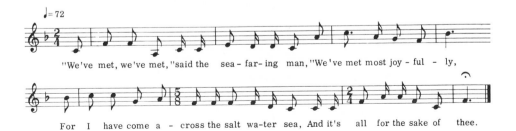

"We've met, we've met," said the sea-far-ing man, "We've met most joy-ful-ly,
For I have come a-cross the salt wa-ter sea, And it's all for the sake of thee.

"We've met, we've met," said the seafaring man,
"We've met most joyfully,
For I have come across the salt water sea,
And it's all for the sake of thee.

"I could have married a king's daughter there,
She offered marriage to me,
But I have come arcoss the salt water sea,
And it's all for the sake of thee."

"If you could have married a king's daughter there,
I'm sure you are to blame,
For I have married a house carpenter,
And I think he's a nice young man."

"Oh, won't you forsake your house carpenter
And go along with me?
I'll take you where the grass grows green
On the banks of the sweet Willie."

She took herself into a room,
And dressed in silk most gay,
And spread a veil all over her face
And outshone the glittering day.

She had not been sailing more'n two weeks,
I'm sure it was not three,
When this fair lady set herself to weeping,
And she wept most bitterly.

"Are you a-weeping for the house carpenter,
Are you a-weeping for fear,
Are you a-weeping for the three little babes
That you left when you come with me here?"

"I'm neither a-weeping for the house carpenter,
I'm neither a-weeping for fear,
I'm only a-weeping for three little babes
That I left when I come with you here."

She had not been sailing more'n three weeks,
I'm sure it was not four,
Till this fair lady threw herself overboard,
And her mourning was heard no more.

He threw himself around three times,
With a dark and dreary eye,
Saying, "The nearest, dearest on earth must part,
And so must you and I."

THE DRUNKARD'S SONG

I learned this song as a child, from the Whites who lived near my family in Lamar County. Mrs. White sang it as I have set it down here. Her two sons, several years older than I, sang it with obscene substitutions for such phrases as "blind old fool." My mother once overheard me singing their words and washed my mouth out with soap and ashes, unwittingly making it certain that the words would stick in my mind. I can still hear them singing, " 'Oh, you fool, you God damned fool, you son-of-a-bitch,' said she."

Sung by Mrs. White, Lamar County, Texas.

An old man came home one night
As drunk as he could be,
And saw a horse standing in the barn
Where his own horse ought to be.

"Oh, my wife, my darling wife,
Now tell me how this can be?
There's somebody's horse standing in the barn
Where my own horse ought to be."

"Oh, you fool, you blind old fool,
Oh, cain't you plainly see?
It's your own brindle cow standing in the barn
Where your own cow ought to be."

"Oh, my wife, my darling wife,
Now tell me how this can be?
There's somebody's hat hanging on the rack
Where my own hat ought to be."

"Oh, you fool, you blind old fool,
Oh, cain't you plainly see?
It's your own black hat hanging on the rack
Where your own hat ought to be."

"Oh, my wife, my darling wife,
Now tell me how this can be?

Somebody's head's in bed with you,
Where my head ought to be."

"Oh, you fool, you blind old fool,
Oh, cain't you plainly see?
It's nothing but a cabbage head
My mother gave to me."

"I've traveled up, I've traveled down,
Ten thousand miles or more,
But hair growing on a cabbage head
I never saw before."

TI RISSLETY ROSSLETY

This song is derived from an English ballad, "The Wife Wrapt in Wether's Skin." In the latter the husband cannot beat his wife, but when she becomes unbearable, he wraps her in a sheepskin and beats the skin until she reforms and becomes a good wife. I have not been able to find a complete version of the ballad in Texas, though the portion printed here is quite well known. In Texas versions the story is lost and the ballad becomes a nonsense song to which singers make up stanzas as they go.

a. Sung by R. R. Denoon, Springfield, Missouri, 1939.

I married me a wife in the month of June,
Risslety Rosslety now now now,
Took her home by the light of the moon.

Refrain:
   Risslety Rosslety hey John dosslety
   Nicklety nacklety
   Rusty koc wally
   Ti willy ti wally ti now now now.

Oh, she swept her floor but once a year,
Risslety Rosslety now now now,
She swore her broom 'twas all too dear.
   (*Refrain*)

Oh, she combs her hair but once a year,
Risslety Rosslety now now now,
At every rake she gives a tear.
   (*Refrain*)

Oh, she churns her butter in dad's old boot,
Risslety Rosslety now now now,
And for her dash she uses her foot.
   (*Refrain*)

Oh, the butter turned to a grizzly gray,
Risslety Rosslety now now now,
The cheese took legs and ran away.
   (*Refrain*)

Oh, the saddle and bridle is on old Jep,
Risslety Rosslety now now now,
You want any more you may sing it yourself.
   (*Refrain*)

b. Sung by Maidy Kelly, Livingston, Texas, 1938.

I married me a wife and I sent her to milk,
Ti rissle ti row row row,
The old crazy thing she didn't know how.

Refrain:
    Ti rissle ti rassle
    Ti how oh, John Dobber,
    Ti Willie, ti Wallie
    Ti Rusty go cwaller
    Ti nickety now now now.

She churns her milk in dad's old boot,
Ti rissle ti row row row,

And for her dasher she uses her foot.
    (*Refrain*)

She takes up her butter in dad's old hat,
Ti rissle ti row row row,
And for her paddle she uses her cat.
    (*Refrain*)

She sweeps her floor but once a year,
Ti rissle ti row row row,
And for her broom she uses her chair.
    (*Refrain*)

THE DEVIL'S SONG

When I was fifteen I worked part of a year as a farm hand for Ulysses S. Swindle of Lamar County. During the summer a young lady named Bessie Baird came to visit from Navarro County. We soon discovered that she knew a song about the devil, but she was afraid to sing it for fear Mr. and Mrs. Swindle would not like it. One night the Swindle children and I got her in the kitchen, closed all the doors and windows, and made her sing the song. I still remember how shocked we were at hearing the line, "If the devil won't have her I'll be damned if I will." I wrote the words down that night and memorized them and the tune.

Many years later I learned that this song, as "The Farmer's Curst Wife," was an old British ballad. The Texas version is quite similar to British versions, except that the language is American and more vigorous.

Sung by William A. Owens.

There was an old man who owned a farm,
Hi Hi diddle um day,
There was an old man who owned a farm,
And he had no cattle to carry it on,
Singing twice fi dum fi diddle fi dum fi day.

He yoked two pigs to pull the plow,
Hi Hi diddle um day,
He yoked two pigs to pull the plow,
And if he did it the devil knows how,
Singing twice fi dum fi diddle fi dum fi day.

The devil came to him in the field one day,
Hi Hi diddle um day,
The devil came to him in the field one day,
Saying, "One of your family I will carry away."
Singing twice fi dum fi diddle fi dum fi day.

"You can't have my oldest son,"
Hi Hi diddle um day,
"You can't have my oldest son,
For the work of the farm must still go on,"
Singing twice fi dum fi diddle fi dum fi day.

"You can have my scolding wife,"
Hi Hi diddle um day,
"You can have my scolding wife,
But you can't keep her to save your life,"
Singing twice fi dum fi diddle fi dum fi day.

He packed her up all in a sack,
Hi Hi diddle um day,
He packed her up all in a sack,
And he looked like a peddler a-packing his pack,
Singing twice fi dum fi diddle fi dum fi day.

Six little devils a-climbing the walls,
Hi Hi diddle um day,
Six little devils a-climbing the walls,
Saying, "Take her back, pappy, 'fore she kills us all,"
Singing twice fi dum fi diddle fi dum fi day.

Six little devils a-dragging their chains,
Hi Hi diddle um day,
Six little devils a-dragging their chains,
Saying, "Take her back, pappy, 'fore she beats out our brains."
Singing twice fi dum fi diddle fi dum fi day.

He packed her up all in a sack,
Hi Hi diddle um day,
He packed her up all in a sack,
And like a damn fool went carrying her back,
Singing twice fi dum fi diddle fi dum fi day.

The old man was lying sick in bed,
Hi Hi diddle um day,
The old man was lying sick in bed,
She took off her shoe and beat him on the head,
Singing twice fi dum fi diddle fi dum fi day.

The old man went whistling across the hill,
Hi Hi diddle um day,
The old man went whistling across the hill,
Saying, "If the devil won't have her I'll be damned if I will,"
Singing twice fi dum fi diddle fi dum fi day.

THE MERRY GOLDEN TREE

I found only this one version of "The Sweet Trinity" or "The Golden Vanity" in Texas, though I have found it in many other places, including an army camp in Australia. The story remains essentially the same through numerous variants, but the "enemy" changes from Turkish to Spanish to Roosian. Only in this version did I find "the Turkish Shivaree," a name no doubt unrelated to the noisy wedding celebrations in rural America.

Sung by Rod Drake, Silsbee, Texas, 1952. There is considerable rhythmic flexibility.

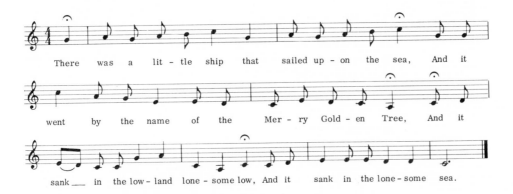

There was a little ship that sailed upon the sea,
And it went by the name of the Merry Golden Tree,
And it sank in the lowland lonesome low,
And it sank in the lonesome sea.

There was another ship that sailed on the sea,
That went by the name of the Turkish Shivaree,
And she sailed on the lowland lonesome low,
And she sailed on the lonesome sea.

"Oh, Captain, oh, Captain, what will you give me
To sink this little ship in the bottom of the sea,
I can sink her in the lowland lonesome low,
I can sink her in the lonesome sea."

"I will give to you money, I'll give to you fee,
Besides my loving daughter I'll marry unto thee,
If you sink her in the lowland lonesome low,
If you sink her in the lonesome sea."

Well, he had a little tool that was made for the use,
That bored nine holes in the bottom at once,
And it sank in the lowland lonesome low,
And it sank in the lonesome sea.

He bowed his head and away swum he
Until he came to the Turkish Shivaree,
And he sunk her in the lowland lonesome low,
And he sunk her in the lonesome sea.

He bowed his head and away swum he
Until he came to the Merry Golden Tree,
That's where he drowned in the lowland lonesome low,
Where he drowned in the lonesome sea.

"Oh, Captain, oh, Captain, take me on board,
For if you don't you have surely broke your word,
And I'll drown in the lowland lonesome low,
And I'll drown in the lonesome sea."

"I won't give you money, I won't give you fee,
And I won't be as good as I said I would be,
You may drown in the lowland lonesome low,
You may drown in the lonesome sea."

"If it wasn't for the love that I have for your men,
I would do unto you as I done unto them,
I would sink you in the lowland lonesome low,
I would sink you in the lonesome sea."

A RICH IRISH LADY

Sometimes known as "Pretty Sally" or "The Brown Girl," this ballad was especially popular with the women in my family, and the cause of considerable discussion at times, as they could never agree on the wording of certain passages. The version printed here was recorded for me by a great-aunt, Mrs. Penelope Haigood. All three versions sung in my family had in the fifth stanza the words "my young Jew," a phrase no one could explain.

The cruelty of the young man can be understood in any Texas community, where a girl's slight is a damaging thing. In some versions the girl did not mean to slight him; she was only slow to respond. But his behavior is the same.

In an English version, called "The Brown Girl," a dark girl is slighted by her lover for a "pretty fair maid." In other details, even to the dancing on the grave, the version printed here follows the English version.

Sung by Mrs. Elizabeth Penelope Haigood, Purcell, Oklahoma, 1938.

A rich Irish lady from London she came,
Fine Sally, fine Sally indeed was her name.
A young man came courting for numbers of years,
Toward this young lady his courtship did steer.

A rich Irish lady from London she came,
Fine Sally, fine Sally indeed was her name.
A young man came courting for numbers of years,
Toward this young lady his courtship did steer.

"Oh, Sally, oh, Sally, and Sally," said he,
"I'm sorry that your love and mine don't agree;
I know that your beauty will my ruin prove
Unless all your hatred will turn unto love."

"Sir, to say that I hate you or any other man,
Or to say that I love you is more than I can;
I neither love you nor hate you, but to end your discourse,
I never will marry you unless I am forced."

Before five and twenty weeks had quickly come and passed,
This young man had heard of her downfall at last.
She sent for this young man all like unto die,
All tangled in love and she knew not for why.

This young man came to her bedside,
Said, "Where lies the pain, in your head or in your side?"
"Oh, no, my young Jew, you cannot know the part;
The pain that troubles me lies nearest my heart."

"Am I any doctor, you sent for me here,
Or am I the young man that once loved you dear?"
"You are the very one that can kill or can cure,
Without your assistance I'll die I am sure."

"Oh, Sally, oh, Sally, and Sally," said he,
"Oh, don't you remember the time you slighted me?
You slighted me, Sally, you slighted me to scorn,
And now I'll reward you, for times past and gone."

"For times past and gone, love, I hope you will forgive,
And grant me yet longer a time here to live."
"I'll never forgive you and while I have breath
I'll dance over your grave when you're cold in the earth."

She took off her fingers gold diamond rings three,
Saying, "Take these and wear them while dancing over me.
I freely forgive you but you cannot me;
Ten thousand times over my folly I see."

ANGLO-AMERICAN BALLADS

FRANCIS JAMES CHILD made his compilation of British popular ballads before collecting folk music became a kind of obsession in America, before competition arose among collectors over which state or region was richest in ballads and ballad variants, before collectors pursued singers up hills and through hollows in hopes of finding a song not reported in some other state. In their zeal these collectors have added broadly to the knowledge of folk song in America. They also found ballads that Child might have included had he known about them. This section will include ballads of probable British origin and then ballads that contain American scenes and themes composed in the British manner.

As demonstrated in the previous section, British ballads could be and were easily adapted to people, places, and incidents in America. The North Country, for instance, became North Carolina. At the same time ballads with few or no identifiable British remnants were being created in America. In subject matter and in names of people and places these ballads are American; in form, textual and musical, they are British, in the manner that British ballads had their form from some earlier people, in an earlier time, in a still undefined location.

In this sense, though there are many ballads that in setting and manner seem wholly American, there is no balladry that is wholly so. In some element or other they are derived from an earlier tradition, cowboy songs included. Substitution of cowboy for sailor does not make a cowboy song; substitution of the gentle rhythm of a galloping pony for the gentle roll of a ship at sea does add an American flavor. A ballad about cowboying, or railroading, or logging demonstrates how easily the ballad can be adapted to the relating of the life experience, whatever it is. Ballads with lines like "We were camped upon the Pecos" and "'Twas in the town of Jacksboro" are not purely Texas. They are too readily transported across the invisible barriers of race and language into the universal. It is this universality that in the long run makes them treasured.

Ballads, whatever their ethnic origin, come and go, in a process by singers of sifting out those that are too regional, too special, or too sentimental. Of the last, the nineteenth century gave America and Texas more than a gracious plenty. Some of those in this section may not withstand erosions of time. Yet they still have a valid comment to make on balladry as a whole.

WILLIAM HALL, OR THE BRISKY YOUNG FARMER

Ballads with happy endings are rare indeed among American singers. The three following are grouped together because they have essentially the same story. It is not a story of mistaken identity so much as a story of no identity at all until the lover who has been absent for years produces a ring or talismanic words that convince his beloved. Then, whether or not the lovers get married, the implication is that they live happily ever after.

a. Sung by Lela Williams, Livingston, Texas, 1938. The first stanza is irregular; the remaining stanzas follow the pattern of the second stanza.

I will tell you of a brisky young farmer
Who has lately gone to the sea;
He courted a fair and handsome lady
Who lived in Desmo town.

And when their parents came for to know this,
They were angry and did say,
"We will send him far across the ocean,
Where his face you'll never more see."

He roamed and roamed the ocean over
Until he came to his native land.
"If Molly is alive and I could find her,
I would make her my lawful wife."

Early, early one morning
As he was walking down the street,
Cold drops of rain fell just as it happened,
For the chance of his true love to meet.

"Good morning, good morning, you pretty fair lady,
Would you choose to fancy me?"
"Oh, no, I fancy a brisky farmer
Who has lately gone to the sea."

"Oh, describe him, oh, describe him,
Oh, describe him unto me;
Perhaps I've seen a sword go through him,
As I've lately crossed the sea."

"My true lover he is handsome,
He is tall and slender too,
His hair is dark and curly,
And his eyes are heavenly blue."

"Oh, yes, I saw him and I knew him,
And his name is William Hall,
And I saw the sword go through him,
And in death I saw him fall."

So she screamed this fair lady,
Saying, "Oh, good Lord, what shall I do?
Oh, now we are parted broken hearted;
Now, good Lord, what shall I do?"

"Cheer up, cheer up, you pretty fair lady,
Cheer up, cheer up," said he;
"And now to convince you of the story,
Here's the ring that you gave me."

Then they joined right hands together,
And straightway to the church did go;
This couple were lawful married
Whether their parents are willing or no.

b. Sung by Rod Drake, Silsbee, Texas, 1952.

Stanzas one, two, six, seven, and eight repeat the last two lines; stanza three repeats the first two lines. The tempo, though it varies somewhat, stays slow and stately.

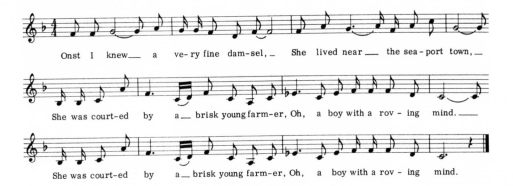

Onst I knew a very fine damsel,
She lived near the seaport town,
She was courted by a brisk young farmer,
Oh, a boy with a roving mind.
She was courted by a brisk young farmer,
Oh, a boy with a roving mind.

When her father came to know that
They were loving each other so
He sailed her across that deep wide ocean.
"Oh, I'll never get to see him anymore."
He sailed her across that deep wide ocean.
"Oh, I'll never get to see him any more."

He re-sailed and he sailed on after her,
Seven long years was he on the sea;
He re-sailed and he sailed on after her,
Seven long years was he on the sea.
"Good morning to my own fair damsel,
Oh, cain't you fancy me?"

"My true love is across the ocean,
Seven long years he's gone to stay;
My true love is across the ocean,
Oh, I'll never get to see him any more."

"Oh, subscribe him, maybe I know him,
For I've lately came from war;
Oh, subscribe him, maybe I know him,
Oh, I've lately came from war."

"He is tall and slim and slender,
His complexion fairly dark,
Has coal black hair and he wears it shingled,
Oh, he's a boy with a roving mind.
Has coal black hair and he wears it shingled,
Oh, he's a boy with a roving mind."

"Yes, I know him, yes, I know him,
For I've lately come from war;
I saw a cannon ball shot through him,
Oh, and a dead man he did fall.
I saw a cannon ball shot through him,
Oh, and a dead man he did fall."

She wrung her hands and hair together,
Crying, "Good Lord, what will I do?
My true love is across that deep wide ocean,
Oh, I'll never get to see him any more.
My true love is across that deep wide ocean,
Oh, I'll never get to see him any more."

He run his hand all in his pocket,
His fingers being slim and small,
Saying, "Here's the ring that you once did give me,
Oh, here's your diamond ring."

They locked hands and walked together,
Through the town and to the church,
And now they're married to each other,
Oh, whether her parents are willing or no.

A PRETTY FAIR MAID

Known as "The Sailor's Return" in English broadsides and as "The Broken Token" in some American versions, "A Pretty Fair Maid" presents a good example of a singer's adaptation of a song's words to make them fit his own background. In England the returned lover is a sailor, in the eastern United States he is a soldier, and in the Southwest he is a cowboy—while the story remains the same throughout, and the word arrangements essentially the same. This song furnishes further proof that the cowboys, instead of creating a new type of ballad literature and music, simply revised the English ballads to suit conditions and traditions in the cow country, or, at best, made up new ballads on patterns already established long ago in England. I know of no other version that mentions Indians.

a. Sung by Miss Willie Haigood and Mrs. Myrtle Woodward, Purcell, Oklahoma, 1938.

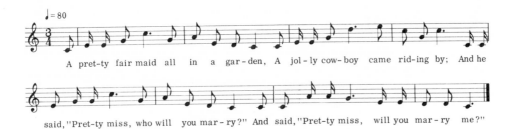

A pretty fair maid all in a garden,
A jolly cowboy came riding by;
And he said, "Pretty miss, who will you marry?"
And said, "Pretty miss, will you marry me?"

"Oh, no, oh, no, my jolly young fellow.
How can you impose on a girl like me?
For I have a true love among the cowboys,
And he's been gone from me seven long years."

"Perhaps your lover he is drownded,
Or perhaps he's by some Indian slain;
Perhaps he's to some pretty girl married,
And you'll never see his face again."

"If he's drownded, I hope he's happy,
Or if he's by some Indian slain,
If he's to some pretty girl married,
I'll love the girl who married him."

He took his hand out of his pocket,
The fingers they were long and slim;
He showed the ring that she had gave him,
And down before him she did fall.

He pressed her close against his bosom,
And gave her kisses one, two, three,
Saying, "If I'd been gone for seven years longer,
No other girl would have married me."

b. Sung by Rod Drake, Silsbee, Texas, 1952. There is variation in tempo.

A pretty fair miss all in the garden,
And a brave young soldier passing by;
He asked her if he could address her;
She made the soldier this reply.

"My true love's gone across the ocean;
Just seven long years he's gone to stay;
And if he stays just seven years longer
No other man can marry me."

"Suppose your true love he got drownded,
Suppose he's in some battle slain,
Suppose he's to some fine girl married,
Whose face on earth you'll never see again."

"Oh, if he's drownded I hope he's happy,
Or if he's in some battle slain,
Or if he's to some fine girl married,
I'll love the girl that married him."

He run his hand all in his pocket,
His fingers being slim and small,
Says, "Here's the ring that you once did give me,"
And down before him she did fall.

He picked her up all in his arms,
And the kisses he give her was one, two, three,
Said, "If I had a-stayed just seven years longer
No girl on earth could have married me."

LATE ONE SUNDAY EVENING

This is an imperfect version of a ballad known in England as "In Bruton Town" and in America as "The Bramble Briar," in which brothers kill their sister's lover to keep him from taking her inheritance. In neither of those versions does the sister drown the two brothers; "Late One Sunday Evening," on the other hand, omits mention of the motive for killing the lover.

Sung by Mrs. Hardy Gore in the Big Thicket of Texas, 1941.

♩ = 76

Late one Sun - day eve - ning as two lov- ers sat talk - ing Her
bro - thers said, "That will not do. Oh we'll take him off in a
game of hunt - ing And noth - ing more shall be found of him."

Late one Sunday evening as two lovers sat talking
Her brothers said, "That will not do.
Oh we'll take him off in a game of hunting
And nothing more shall be found of him."

And the very next day they started out walking,
They walked over hills and over valleys,
Until they came to some lonesome valley,
And there they left him a-lying dead.

And the very next day when they returned home
Their sister asked them where was he.
"Oh, he was lost in a game of hunting,
And nothing more shall be found of him."

And the very next day she started out walking;
She walked over hills and over valleys
Until she came to some lonesome valley,
And there she found him a-lying dead.

She stooped over him and kissed him, crying,
Saying, "Now hungry is a-calling me home;
For I've been roving three days and nights
And now hungry is a-calling me home."

And the very next day when she returned home
Her brothers asked her where was she.
"Oh, hold your tongues, you trifling villains,
For you both shall hang for the sake of one."

And the very next day she pushed them both unto the ocean,
And they both had a watery grave;
And the wind did blow and the leaves did shadow,
And they both had a watery grave.

LOVELY WILLIAM

The words and tune of this song printed here were given me by May Kennedy McCord of Springfield, Missouri. She had never heard all of the song. I have found people in the Big Thicket who vaguely remembered the story. Peter Bell of Carrizo Springs knew the tune with only slight variations, but he could not give the words. The story in general is that the father lay in ambush (an explanation of "lies in lust") for the young couple to return at night. When they came to a certain tree in the garden he killed the young man with his dagger.

The song is probably of English origin, though I have not been able to find any record of it.

Sung by May Kennedy McCord, Springfield, Missouri, 1939.

The reason for using 6/4 meter in this song is to demonstrate that all the lines are equal in length (six beats) and that rhythmic and melodic structure correspond very closely.

"There's a tree in father's garden,
Lovely William," says she;
"Where young men and young maidens,
They wait there for me;
Where my father lies in lust
Brave deeds for to do."
With a long and silver dagger
He pierced his love through.

ONCE I COURTED A FAIR BEAUTY BRIDE

Sung by Mrs. Dock Eason in the Big Thicket in Southeast Texas.

The singer omits lines two and four of the first stanza. She sings the music for lines one and two to the words of lines one and three. From stanza two on, the music and text are regular. (For this reason the words of stanza two are placed with the music, instead of those of stanza one.) There are wide variations in tempo from stanza to stanza. In general, the singer begins slowly and ends faster.

Once I courted a fair beauty bride,
And on her I fixed my whole heart's delight;
I courted her for love, and love did attain,
Which I never had a reason at all to complain.

Her old cruel father came somehow to know
That me and his daughter loved one another so;
He put her in a parlor, in a parlor so bright,
And I never seen my love alone once more.

Up to her window that I desired to go,
To see if I could see my loved one at all,
When I got there, she wrang her hands and cried,
Saying, "I love the man that loves me and I'll love him till I die."

Off to the army that I desired to go,
To see if I could forget my loved one at all,
When I got there, the army shone so bright
Till it made me think of my own heart's delight.

Seven long years that I served as a king;
Seven long years I returned home again;
When I got there, her mother wrang her hands and cried,
Saying, "My daughter loved you dearly and for your sake she died."

There I stood like a lamb to be slain;
Tears from my eyes like showers of rain;
Saying, "Come, young people, come pity pity me,
Come pity my misfortune and I'll pity thee."

When I came to my senses again,
Pen and ink and a copy of the same;
Saying, "Come, young people, come pity pity me,
Come pity my misfortune and I'll pity thee."

COME ALL YOU PRETTY FAIR MAIDS

This song, first printed in 1816, shows its origin in some traditional British symbolism: thyme for virginity, primrose for carefree love, willow for sorrow. My first acquaintance with it was in 1936, when it was sung by May Kennedy McCord at the National Folk Festival in Dallas, Texas. In 1941 Rod Drake sang but did not record an almost identical version at Fred, Texas. Peter Bell of Carrizo Spring, Texas, also remembered one stanza and the melody from his father's singing.

Sung by May Kennedy McCord, Springfield, Missouri, 1939.

The rhythmic organization is based on the poetic structure, which is similar to that of "The Little Sparrow."

Come all you pretty fair maids
Who flourish in your prime;
Be sure you keep your garden clean;
Let no one take your thyme.

In June grows the primrose,
But it's no flower for me;

I'll pluck up my primrose
And plant a willow tree.

Green willow I'll wear, love,
With sorrow mixed among
To show to all the world
That I loved a false young man.

THE LITTLE SPARROW

This is possibly a fragment of an old ballad, the remainder of which has been lost; no complete version has been reported in either England or the United States. The theme of the forsaken girl appears all through ballad literature. So does that of the person who wishes to transform himself into a sparrow or a dove and fly to the side of the loved one.

This song is widely known in the United States. I found two persons in the Big Thicket area who could sing it, and Peter Bell of Carizzo Springs played it on the fiddle.

Sung by May Kennedy McCord, Springfield, Missouri, 1939. The chords are from the singer's guitar accompaniment.

Come, all you fair and ten - der la - dies, Take warn-ing how you treat your men; They're like a star in a cloud - y morn-ing; At first they're here and then they're gone.

This song, though without meter or steady pulse, has a consistent rhythmic organization based on verse accent and melodic structure. Three short syllables form a kind of upbeat to the longest and highest note of each line; each line also has a second accented syllable, slightly less important than the first:

> Come all you | FAIR and | *ten*der ladies,
> Take warning | HOW you | *treat* your men;
> They're like a | STAR in a | *clou*dy morning;
> At first they're | HERE and | *then* they're gone.

Come, all you fair and tender ladies,
Take warning how you treat your men;
They're like a star in a cloudy morning;
At first they're here and then they're gone.

They'll tell to you some lonesome story,
They'll prove to you their love is true,
And then they'll go and court another—
Oh, that is the love they have for you.

I wish I was a little sparrow,
And I had wings and I could fly;
I'd fly away to my false lover,
And there I'd sit me down and cry.

But I am not a little sparrow;
I have no wings and cannot fly;
So I'll lay me down in my grief and sorrow,
I'll lay me down until I die.

I DREAMED LAST NIGHT OF MY TRUE LOVE

Sung by Rod Drake, Silsbee, Texas, 1952.

I dreamed last night of my true love,
All in my arms I held her;
Her curly hair like strands of gold
Was dangling on my pillow.

When I awoke it was not so;
I was forced to lie there without her;
When I awoke it was not so;
I was forced to lie without her.

I got up next morning and saddled my horse,
I lonesome hills to ride over;
I got up next morning and saddled my horse,
I lonesome hills to ride over.

I rode up to her uncle's gate
Inquiring of my jewel.
Her uncle came out with this reply,
"I know nothing about her."

I got down and walked into the yard;
I heard my jewel moaning;
I got down and walked into the yard;
I heard my jewel moaning.

There was nothing there but locks and bolts,
But locks and bolts to hinder.
I split a lock, I broke a bolt,
I driv them all to shadows.

I takened my jewel by her hand,
I led her out right amongst them.
"If there's anyone here has more right than me,
Take one and fight the other."

COME, ALL YOU JOLLY COWBOYS

Sung by Rod Drake, Silsbee, Texas, 1952.

Slow, without measure

Come, all you jol-ly cow-boys, bound on — a storm-y land, I'll tell — to you some trou-ble — that's hap-pened to me, I left my home and friends so dear — to roam the prai-rie plain, And — now — I have to leave you all — to nev-er re-turn a-gain. And did-n't my mo-ther's voice trem-ble, — say-ing, "Child, oh, child, I fear Some ac-ci-dent might hap-pen — and I could — not meet you there." A maid so fair and love-ly grew close-ly to my side, And there she pro-mised faith-ful-ly — that she — would be my bride. I kissed her with these flow-ing tears that fill-ed her blue eyes — My heart has nev-er grown cold-er — and my love — has nev-er died.

Line:	1	2	3	4	5	6	7	8	9	10
Text:	a	b	c	c	d	e	f	f	g	f
Music:	A	B	A	B'	C	A	C	A	C	A

The irregular rhyme scheme and pattern of musical repetition indicates that this is a fragment of a song whose integral form cannot be determined.

The present system of dividing the lines makes the musical form clear, but it obscures rhythmic structure. If the lines, which vary in length from twelve to sixteen syllables, are divided into shorter lines, each with three or four strong accents, it becomes easier to perceive a rhythmic organization based on verse accent.

Come, all you jolly cowboys, bound on a stormy land,
I'll tell to you some trouble that's happened to me,
I left my home and friends so dear to roam the prairie plain,
And now I have to leave you all to never return again.

And didn't my mother's voice tremble, saying, "Child, oh, child, I fear
Some accident might happen and I could not meet you there."
A maid so fair and lovely grew closely to my side,
And there she promised faithfully that she would be my bride.

I kissed her with these flowing tears that filléd her blue eyes—
My heart has never grown colder and my love has never died.

ON THE RED RIVER SHORE

Sung by Rod Drake, Silsbee, Texas, 1952. There is considerable rhythmic flexibility.

On the foot of yonders mountain where the cannons do roar,
Sweet music enterticed me while the south wind doth blow,
I spied a fair damsel a-walking alone,
A-walking all alone on the Red River Shore.

Her stout-hearted father, those words he did hear;
He says, "I will advise you of the dearest, oh, dear."

He drew a large army, some twenty or more,
To fight her own true love on the Red River Shore.

He drew a long sword around and around;
Some of them was wounded, and some of them was slain.
"Hold up," says the old man, "Don't fight so brave.
You have courted for my army to be carried to the grave."

[*Line 1 and 2 missing.*]
"Hold up," says the old man, "don't fight no more.
You can have your own true love on the Red River Shore."

LOVELY MARY

Sung by Rod Drake, Silsbee, Texas, 1952.

The singer breaks the regularity of the moderately paced quarter-note pulse to emphasize important syllables, indicated here by a fermata (⌢).

It was on last Sunday evening
My love she passed me by;
I saw her mind was changing
By the movements of her eye.

I saw her mind was changing
To some other high degree.
Says I to Lovely Mary,
"Why cain't you fancy me?

"Why cain't you fancy me?
Why cain't you fancy me?"

As I told Lovely Mary,
"Why cain't you fancy me?"

Her hair was as black as a raven,
Her eyes were as black as a crow,
Her cheeks were like red roses
All in the morning glow;

All in the morning glow,
All in the morning glow,
Her cheeks was like red roses
All in the morning glow.

I wisht I was in Babylon
Or some other seaport town;
I'd set my foot on aboard a ship,
I'd sail the ocean round.

I'd sail the ocean round,
I'd sail the ocean round,
I'd set my foot on aboard a ship,
I'd sail the ocean round.

While sailing over the ocean,
While sailing over the sea,
I'd think of Lovely Mary
Before I went to sleep.

Before I went to sleep,
Before I went to sleep,
I'd think of Lovely Mary
Before I went to sleep.

AS I WALKÉD OUT ON A MAY MORNING

Sung by Rod Drake, Silsbee, Texas, 1952.

In the second, fourth, fifth, and sixth stanzas, the last two lines are repeated. There is flexibility in tempo and rhythm.

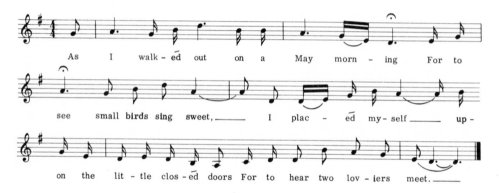

As I walkéd out on a May morning
For to see small birds sing sweet,
I placéd myself upon the little closéd doors
For to hear two loviers meet.

For to see two loviers meet, my love,
And to hear what they had for to say
That I might have learned a little more that they had for to say
Before I went away,
That I might have learned a little more that they had for to say
Before I went away.

Oh, come ye here, my own true love,
And set you down upon my knee
And let me learn a little more that you have for to say
Before I go away.

Well, I won't git down, and I shan't sit down,
For I have not a moment of time,

For I heard that you had you another true love
And your heart is no more mine,
For I heard that you had you another sweetheart
And your love it is no more mine.

Well, I hope to climb as high a pine
And to rob as rich a nest
And then I hope for to come down again
And marry the one that I love best,
And then I hope for to come down again,
And to marry the one that I love best.

Well, I never will believe what a young man says
Neither in a city or a town,
Unless that he is upon some high gallows top
And he says that he will come down,
Unless that he is upon some high gallows top
And he says that he will come down.

ALL IN THE SCENES OF WINTER

Sung by Rod Drake, Silsbee, Texas, 1952.

All in the scenes of winter
The times of frost and snow,
Dark clouds a-hov'ring around me—
How chilly the wind doth blow.

I went to see my true love,
She fooled most scornfully;
I asked her to marry me
And she would not answer me.

"The night is almost over, love,
It's now the break of day,
I'm waiting for an answer,
Kind love, what do you say?"

"If an answer you are waiting for
I choose a single life;
I never thought it suited
For me to be your wife."

In the course of two weeks past or three
This lady's mind did change,
She wrote him a letter,
"Kind sir, I feel ashamed."

He answered her kind letter,
He said it in despair,
"I once loved you dearly,
Yes, dearly indeed.

"But since you have offended me   "The birds is singing sweet, my love,
I'll look some other way;   On every bush and vine,
I'll never look upon you   My troubles would be over
Until my dying day.   If you would only mind."

I WAS OUT WALKING

Sung by Rod Drake, Silsbee, Texas, 1952.

I was out walking, out walking one day,
I met a fair couple a-making their way,
And one was a lady and a fair one was she,
And the other'n was a cowboy and a brave one was he,
And the other'n was a cowboy and a brave one was he.

"Oh, where are you going, my pretty fair maid?"
"I'm a-going to the river, just down by the spring,
I'm a-going to the river, just down by the spring,
To see the water gliding, hear the nightingale sing,
To see the water gliding, hear the nightingale sing."

They had not been down there more than an hour or two
Before out of a satchel a fiddle he drew;
He played them a lexture which made it fairly ring.
"Hark, hark," said the fair maid, "hear the nightingale sing,
"Hark, hark," says the fair maid, "hear the nightingale sing."

"Oh, now," said this cowboy, "it's time I was gone."
"No, no," says the fair maid, "just play one more tune.
I'd rather hear a fiddle just picked on one string

Than to see the water gliding, hear the nightingale sing,
Than to see the water gliding, hear the nightingale sing."

"Oh, now," says this fair maid, "won't you marry me?"
"No, no," says the cowboy, "that never can be.
I have a wife in old Mexico, children two or three,
Two women on a cow range, too many for me,
Two women on a cow range, too many for me."

"I'll go to old Mexico, I'll stay there one year,
I'll drink cold spring water for the distillments of beer,
And if I come back here it'll be in the spring,
To see the water gliding, hear the nightingale sing,
To see the water gliding, hear the nightingale sing."

"Oh, now," says this fair maid, "take warning by me,
Don't place your affections on a cowboy so gay,
For yours will leave you like mine left me
To rockabye cradle, sing byo baby,
To rockabye cradle, sing byo baby."

OH, WILLIE

Sung by Rod Drake, Silsbee, Texas, 1952.

Rhythmic organization is based on the structure of the poetic line. Each line has two equal sections in which three weak beats precede the primary accent: "Oh, Willie, oh, WILLIE,‖ I love you WELL."

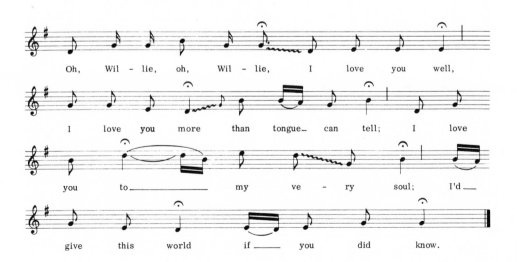

Oh, Willie, oh, Willie, I love you well,
I love you more than tongue can tell;
I love you to my very soul;
I'd give this world if you did know.

When her old father came to know
That Willie and Jewel was loving so
He whipped and tore them one and all
And swore he'd use a cannon ball.

When her old father came home at night
Inquiring of Jewel, his heart's delight,

Upstairs he went, a door he broke,
He found her hanging by her own dead
    rope.

He out with his knife and he cut her down,
And on her breast this note was found,
"Go dig my grave both deep and wide,
And bury my darling by my side."

He read this note and wept and said,
"Lord, ain't it a pity that I was dead."
He read the note and wept and said,
"I wish ten times that I were dead."

YOUNG JOHNNIE

This ballad, as "The Green Bed," is widely known in England and Scotland. It has been reported in the United States as "Jackson," "Jack Tar," and "The Liverpool Landlady."

Mrs. Ben Dryden of Sandy Creek settlement called it "an old fool song" when she sang it for me. Her version is quite similar to others reported in America.

a. Sung by Mrs. Ben Dryden, Fred, Texas, 1941.

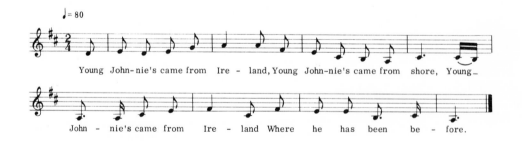

Young Johnnie's came from Ireland,
Young Johnnie's came from shore,
Young Johnnie's came from Ireland,
Where he has been before.

"It's what's for luck, young Johnnie?"
"It's very bad," says he.
"I lost my ship and cargo
All on the raging sea.

"Bring down your daughter Polly
And set her on my knee;
We'll drown the melancholy
And married we will be."

"My daughter Polly's absent,
She ain't been seen today,
And if she were here, John,
She'd turn you out of door.

"Without this companion
You're turned out of door;
Without this companion
You're turned out of door."

Young Johnnie, feeling drowsy,
He hung down his head;
Inquiring for a candle
To light him to the bed.

"Your great bed is full of strangers
And has been weeks or more,
And without this companion
You're turned out of door."

Young Johnnie, feeling drowsy,
He leant from the wall;
He looked upon the people,
He looked upon them all.

There were thirty of them new,
And forty of the old;

Young Johnnie pulled out his
Two hands full of gold.

His daughter Polly came
Down that-a-way,
She laid her arms around him
And did him embrace.

"You're welcome home, young Johnnie,
You're welcome home from the sea;
Your great bed is empty
And you shall lodge there."

"It's when I had no money
My lodging was the sea;
But plenty of money
I'll lodge where I please.

"Before I'd lodge there
I'd lodge in the street
With a bottle of peach brandy
And on my knee a girl."

b. Sung by Rod Drake, Silsbee, Texas, 1952.

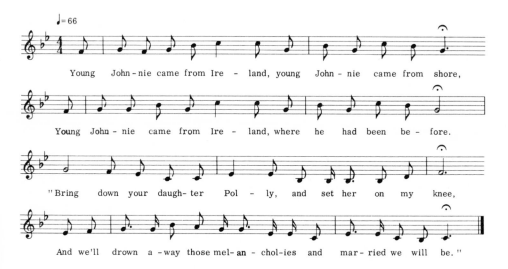

Young Johnnie came from Ireland, young Johnnie came from shore,
Young Johnnie came from Ireland, where he had been before.
"Bring down your daughter Polly, and set her on my knee,
And we'll drown away those melancholies and married we will be."

"What's the luck, young Johnnie?" "Awful bad," says he,
"I lost my ship and cargo all on the raging sea.

Bring down your daughter Polly, and set her on my knee,
And we'll drown away those melancholies and married we will be."

"My daughter Polly's absent, she hasn't been seen today,
[*Line 2 missing.*]
And Polly being rich, John, and you so very poor,
And if she was at home she would turn you out of door."

Young Johnnie feeling tired he hung down his head,
He called for a candle to light him to bed.
"Your bed is full of strangers, John, and have been weeks or more,
And you'll have to seek your lodging and some other shore."

Young Johnnie feeling tired, he leant from against the wall,
He looked among the people, he looked among them all.
There was forty of the young, and fifty of the old,
And out of his pockets he pulled both hands full of gold.

Young Polly came home and she went down that way,
She threw her arms around him, and did him embrace.
"Your great bed is empty, John, and have been weeks or more,
Your great bed is empty and you may lie there."

"Before I would lie there I'd lodge in the street,
It's when I had no money my lodging were at sea;
And now I've plenty of money I'll seek the tavern door,
And before I would lodge there I'd lodge out of doors."

THE OXFORD GIRL

This song dates back with me to the age of five, when my family moved to a community on the blackland in the southern part of Lamar County. My older brothers learned the ballad from our new neighbors; I memorized the entire song and frequently sang it while at play. My love of it was probably comparable to the current love of children for the blood and violence of comic books. I can remember with what pleasure I sang the lines

> I picked her up by the long yellow hair
> And slung her round and round;
> I took her to the Oxford stream
> And plunged her in to drown.

This ballad was originally an English broadside called "The Berkshire Tragedy, or The Wittam Miller." It was published in America in the nineteenth century as a penny song sheet with the title "The Lexington Miller."

Sung by William A. Owens.

'Twas in the town of Ox - ford That I did live and dwell;

'Twas in the town of Ox - ford I owned a flour_____ mill.

'Twas in the town of Oxford
That I did live and dwell;
'Twas in the town of Oxford
I owned a flour mill.

I fell in love with an Oxford girl
With dark and rolling eyes;
I asked her if she'd marry me;
She said she'd never deny.

I told her that we'd take a walk
Out in the meadows gay;
I told her that we'd take a talk
And name the wedding day.

We walked along and we talked along
Till we came to level ground;
I up with a hand and stick
And fairly knocked her down.

She fell upon her bended knees,
Crying, "Willie, please spare my life;
Oh, Willie, my dear, don't murder me,
For I'm not prepared to die."

I did not listen to her cry
But beat her more and more;
I beat her until her body lay
A-bleeding in the gore.

I picked her up by the long yellow hair
And slung her round and round;
I took her to the Oxford stream
And plunged her in to drown.

"Lie there, lie there, you Oxford girl,
You never will be my bride;
Lie there, lie there, you Oxford girl,
You never will be my bride."

When I got home at twelve that night
My mother woke in fright;
"Oh, Willie, my son, what have you done
To bloody your hands tonight?"

I asked her for a candle
To light my way to bed;
I asked for a handkerchief
To bind my aching head.

'Twas in the town of Oxford
That Oxford girl was found,
A-floating down the Oxford stream
That flows through Oxford town.

"Oh, mother, they're going to hang me
Between the earth and sky;
Oh, mother, they're going to hang me,
And I'm not prepared to die."

THE DRUMMER BOY OF WATERLOO

Many a night when I was a child I grew sad as my mother and grandmother
sang this ballad. They never knew the real meaning of Waterloo, and apparently

connected it with the Civil War; at least it would always set my grandmother to telling her own Civil War experiences and stories of battle she had heard. "The Drummer Boy of Shiloh," a Civil War song my family never knew, was probably based on this song, though the relationship is barely recognizable.

"The Drummer Boy of Waterloo" was a popular broadside in England and was published as a penny song sheet in America.

Sung by William A. Owens.

When bat-tle round each war-like band With cour-age loud the trum-pet blew,

Young Ed-ward left his na-tive land, A drum-mer boy of Wa-ter-loo.

When battle round each warlike band	They marched until the set of sun,
With courage loud the trumpet blew,	Beheld the army's force subdue;
Young Edward left his native land,	The flash of death, the murderer's gun
A drummer boy of Waterloo.	That laid him low at Waterloo.
Young Edward knew no infant fears,	They placed his head upon his drum
His knapsack over his shoulder threw.	Beneath the moonlight's mournful hue.
He cried, "Dear mother, dry those tears	"Comrades, comrades," Edward cried,
Till I return from Waterloo."	"Adieu, adieu, adieu to you."
Then his lips his mother pressed	They fired three rounds across his grave
And bid her noble boy adieu;	In token of their fallen brave;
With wringing hands and aching breast,	The echoes rang from shore to shore,
Beheld him march for Waterloo.	"Young Edward's gone for ever more."

YOUNG CHARLOTTIE

The authorship of this ballad has been traced by Phillips Barry (*Journal* 25:156) to a nineteenth-century New York journalist named Seba Smith, who under the pseudonym of Major Jack Downing wrote satires on Jacksonian democracy. The language, though rather literary for a folk ballad, has been only slightly altered in over a hundred years of oral circulation: the stanzas presented here, which I learned from my mother, are remarkably like the earliest printed versions. My mother apparently did not know the final stanza of the original, a bit of moralizing on pride.

Sung by William A. Owens.

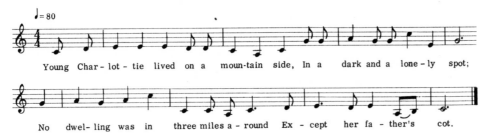

Young Char-lot-tie lived on a moun-tain side, In a dark and a lone-ly spot;

No dwel-ling was in three miles a-round Ex-cept her fa-ther's cot.

Young Charlottie lived on a mountain side,
In a dark and lonely spot;
No dwelling was in three miles around,
Except her father's cot.

And many a lonely winter's night
Young swains would gather there;
Her father kept a social abode,
And she was very fair.

On New Year's Eve, the sun gone down,
With a dark and a wistful eye
Young Charlottie sat by her father's door
To watch the sleighs go by.

But brightly beamed her restless eye,
As his well-known voice she heard;
Come driving up to the cottage door,
Young Charlie's sleigh appeared.

"There is a merry ball tonight
Just fifteen miles away;
The air is freezing cold as death,
But our hearts are light and gay."

"Charlottie, dear," her mother said,
"This blanket around you fold,
For it's a dreadful night outside,
And you'll catch your death of cold."

"Oh, no, no, no," Charlottie said,
For she felt like a gypsy queen,
"To ride in a blanket muffled up
I never would be seen.

"My silken cloak is enough for me,
It's lined, you know, throughout;

And here I have my silken scarf
To tie my neck about."

Her bonnet and her scarf were on,
She stepped into the sleigh;
Away they rode to the mountain side
And o'er the hills away.

"It's a dreadful night," young Charlie said,
"The reins I scarce can hold."
Then Charlottie said in these few words,
"I am exceeding cold."

He cracked his whip, he urged his team
Much faster than before,
Until five more merry miles
In silence they passed o'er.

"How fast," said Charlie, "The ice and snow
Are freezing on my brow."
Then Charlottie said in these few words,
"I'm growing warmer now."

They drove along in the frosty air
And in the cold starlight,
Until at length at the village ball
They both appeared in sight.

He drove to the door and then jumped out,
He gave to her his hand;
He asked her for her hand again,
But still she did not stir.

He took her by the lily-white hand,
It was cold and hard as stone;
He lifted the scarf from off her brow,
While the stars above them shone.

Then quickly to the lighted hall
Her lifeless corpse he bore;
Young Charlottie was frozen to death
And she never spoke no more.

He twined his arms around her neck,
He kissed her marble brow,
While his thoughts went back to where she
    said,
"I'm growing warmer now."

THE BUTCHER'S BOY

When I was a child "The Butcher's Boy" was a favorite song at school and at musical entertainments in homes. Even in our own community there were slight variations in words and tune. The location was sometimes London City, sometimes Jersey City. The final stanza, however, rarely showed variation.

This song appeared as a broadside in England and as a penny song sheet in America. It is known throughout the United States.

Sung by May Kennedy McCord, Springfield, Missouri, 1939. The chords are from the singer's guitar accompaniment.

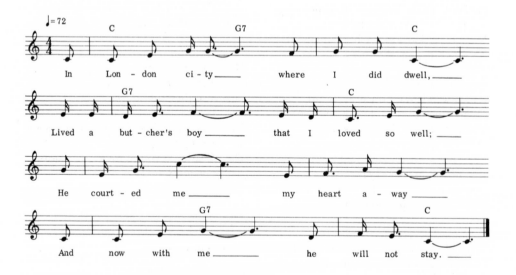

In London city where I did dwell,
Lived a butcher's boy that I loved so well;
He courted me my heart away
And now with me he will not stay.

There is a house in London town
Where my true love goes and he dares sit down;
He takes a strange girl on his knee
And he tells to her what he won't tell me.

"Oh, mother, mother, I'll tell you why—
It's because she has more gold than I;
But her gold will melt and her silver fly,
And she will be as poor as I."

Her father come home from a far-off town,
Saying, "Where, oh, where is my daughter gone?"
Saying, "Where, oh, where is my pride and joy?
Oh, has she gone with the butcher's boy?"

He went upstairs, the door he broke,
And found her hanging by a rope;
He took a knife and cut her down,
And on her bosom these lines he found:

"Go dig my grave both wide and deep,
Place a marble stone at my head and feet,
And on my breast place a turtle dove
To show to the world that I died for love.

"Must I go bound while he goes free?
Must I love a man who don't love me?
Oh, I have played a maiden's part
And died for the man who broke my heart."

THE WILD MOOR

From this version it is difficult to piece together a coherent story. Apparently Mary, "once the gay village bride," and her baby had been deserted by her husband. She came home to her father, but because of his deafness was unable to awaken him. She died of the cold, he of grief, and the baby of neglect. The cottage, regarded as haunted, goes to ruin.

This ballad was published as a penny song sheet about 1860. Possibly it was taken from the English version. It has been reported from several sections of the United States; I have found it in the Missouri Ozarks as well as in Southeast Texas.

Sung by Benjamin F. Rice, Springfield, Missouri, 1939.

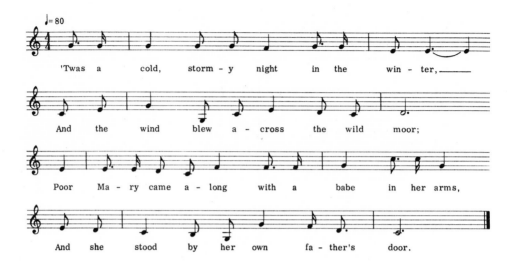

'Twas a cold, stormy night in the winter,
And the wind blew across the wild moor;
Poor Mary came along with a babe in her arms,
And she stood by her own father's door.

"Oh, father, dear father," she cried,
"Come down, please, and open the door,
For the babe in my arms will perish and die
By the wind that sweeps o'er the wild moor."

The old man being deaf to her cries,
Not one sound of her voice reached his ears;
But the dogs they did bark and the village bells tolled
By the wind that sweeps o'er the wild moor.

Oh, what did the old man think
When he come to the door in the morn?
Poor Mary was dead but the babe still alive,
Closely pressed in its dead mother's arms.

The old man in grief pined away,
And the babe to its mother went soon;
And no one they say has lived there till this day,
And the cottage to ruins has gone.

The villagers point out the spot
Where the willows droop over the door,
Saying, "There Mary died, once the gay village bride,
By the wind that sweeps o'er the wild moor."

LITTLE MOHEA

George Lyman Kittredge believed "Little Mohea" was a remaking of an English ballad called "The Indian Lass"—a broadside popular in America about the middle of the nineteenth century. "The Indian Lass" as printed by DeMarsan in 1860 does have the same story, but the words are quite different, as the following lines indicate:

> She was neat, tall and handsome, her age was 16,
> Was born and brought up in a place near Orleans.

Eckstorm and Smith (*Minstrelsy of Maine*), on the other hand, are of the opinion that "Little Mohea" was originally a sailor song and that Mohea is a reference to Maui of the Sandwich Islands, which the old explorers called Mohea. Their theory successfully explains the use of the phrases "coconut grove" and "South Sea" in the version printed here, as recorded by Mrs. C. H. Burke of Silsbee. As a matter of fact, this is the only version I have seen naming the South Sea as the location of the song, which was popular during my childhood and is still widely known in Texas.

Sung by Mrs. C. H. Burke, Silsbee, Texas, 1938.

This song, although it is not in either a common duple or triple meter, has a regularity based on the steady eight-note pulse (♪ 150) and the musical and textual symmetry in all the lines.

The pattern of musical repetition for the third stanza is A A B A B C.

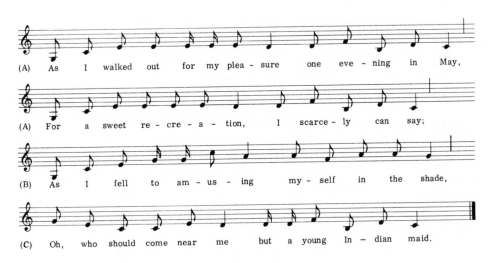

As I walked out for my pleasure one evening in May,
For a sweet recreation, I scarcely can say;
As I fell to amusing myself in the shade,
Oh, who should come near me but a young Indian maid.

She sat down beside me, and taking my hand,
Says she, "You are a stranger, not one of our band,
But if you will follow you're welcome to come
And share in my cottage, the humblest of homes."

The sun was fast sinking far o'er the blue sea,
When I was a-rambling with my pretty Mohea;
Together we wandered, together we roamed,
Till we came to a log hut in a coconut grove.

With kindly expressions she said unto me,
"If you will consent, sir, and live here with me,
And go no more rambling all o'er the South Sea;
I'll teach you the language of the little Mohea."

"Oh, no, pretty maiden, this never can be;
I have a true lover all o'er the South Sea;
I could not forsake her and live here with thee,
For her heart beats as true as the little Mohea."

This fair young lady, she's handsome and kind,
She acted her part as though heaven designed,
For I was a stranger and she took me to her home,
And I think of little Mohea as I wander alone.

The last time I saw her she stood on the sand
As our ship passed by her she waved me her hand,
Saying, "When you get back to the girl that you love,
Just think of little Mohea in the coconut grove."

Now I am safe landed on Hudson's green shore,
Where my friends and companions can view me once more;
The girls all crowd around me, but none do I see
That can compare with my little Mohea.

THE JEALOUS LOVER

Thomas Hart Benton's painting "The Jealous Lover of Lone Green Valley" has helped to immortalize this song—if it needed any help. During my period of ballad collecting in Texas I heard it numberless times as "Florella," "Flora Ella," "Lurella," "Pearl Bryan," and "Pearl Brown," proof enough that the folks themselves have marked it for their own special kind of immortality. Though it bears little similarity to the tale of Florella, the story of Pearl Bryan, a real person who was murdered sensationally on February 1, 1896, near Fort Thomas, Kentucky, caught the folk imagination and has been attached to one version of the older ballad.

Sung by Opal Patton, Austin, Texas, 1939. The chords are from the singer's guitar accompaniment.

Down in a lone - ly val - ley Where the vio - lets gent - ly bloom, —

Flor - el - la lies for - got - ten In a cold and si - lent tomb. —

Down in a lonely valley
Where the violets gently bloom,
Florella lies forgotten
In a cold and silent tomb.

She died not broken hearted,
Nor in sickness did she fail,
But in one moment parted
From the ones she loved so dear.

One night as the moon shone brightly
And lightly fell the dew,
Down to her lonely cottage
A jealous lover drew.

"Florella, let us wander
Down by a meadow gay;
There let us sit and ponder
Upon our wedding day."

The way was cold and dreary,
The night was coming on;
Into that lonely valley
He led the maiden on.

"Oh, Edward, I'm so weary,
Wandering here so long.

The night is cold and dreary,
I pray you take me home."

"You have not the wings of an angel,
Nor from me can you fly;
You cannot now escape me,
Florella, you must die."

Down, down on her knees she bended
And begged him for her life,
But into her snowy white bosom
He plunged a gleaming knife.

"Oh, Edward, I forgive you
With all my dying breath;
I never have deceived you,
As I close my eyes in death."

Down, down on his knees he bended,
Saying, "What have I done?
I've murdered my own Florella,
True as the rising sun."

Down in that lonely valley
Where the willows weep o'er her grave,
Florella lies forgotten
Where the merry sunbeams play.

THE BANKS OF CLODDIE

Though this ballad does not appear in the Child collection, it is well known in England, Scotland, and Ireland, and is no doubt of British origin. It was published as a penny song sheet by Johnson's Cheap Printing Office in Philadelphia

about 1860, and was frequently parodied by minstrel singers. Several persons in
Texas have sung it for me.

"The Banks of Cloddie" is closely related to "The Banks of the Nile," an Irish
song of uncertain origin, in which young Jimmy is being sent to fight the Arabs in
Egypt. His wife Nancy begs to go with him, saying that she will cut off her hair
and fight beside him. His reply is

> Oh, say not so, dear Nancy,
> For that you can not do.
> Our Colonel he has ordered
> No women there can go.
> The blazing sun of Egypt
> Your beauty soon would spoil,
> And your bones would lie a-bleaching
> On the banks of the Nile.

He leaves her alone, and in the last stanza we discover the end of the story.

> Farewell to the banks of Clowdy—
> The scene of all my joy.
> Farewell to the banks of Clowdy,
> Where I met my darling boy.
> He would take me in his arms
> And his tender eyes would smile—
> Now his body lies a-mold'ring
> On the banks of the Nile.

"The Banks of the Nile" was published as a penny song sheet early in the
nineteenth century, but I have not run across it in Texas.

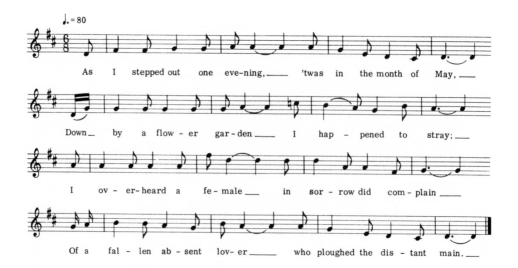

As I stepped out one evening, 'twas in the month of May,
Down by a flower garden I happened to stray;
I overheard a female in sorrow did complain
Of a fallen absent lover who ploughed the distant main.

I stepped up to her, I took her on surprise;
I knew she wouldn't know me, for I was in disguise.
"Oh, where are you going, my own heart's delight?
Oh, where are you going this dark and rainy night?"

"I'm hunting for a young man, young Johnnie is his name;
On the banks of Cloddie I'm told he does remain;
On the banks of Cloddie, if you would please to show
And pity a poor female, for there I'm bound to go."

"On the banks of Cloddie on which you now do stand;
But never mind young Johnnie, for he's a false young man;
Oh, never mind young Johnnie, for he'll not need you here;
Just stay with me in the greenwood, no danger need you fear."

"If Johnnie was here this night he'd carry me from all harm,
But he's on the field of battle dressed in his uniform;
He's on the field of battle for honor and great gain—"
"The ship's been wrecked so I've been told all on her way from Spain."

When she heard this dreadful news she fell into despair
With wringing of her hands and tearing of her hair,
Saying, "If young Johnnie's dead, no other will I take,
Through the lonesome hills and valleys I'll ramble for his sake."

When I heard this joyful news, I could no longer stand;
I caught her in my arms, saying, "Mollie, I'm the man."
Saying, "Mollie, I'm the man that's caused you all this pain,
And since we've met on Cloddie's banks we'll never part again."

FAIR FANNIE MOORE

When I was a child my mother frequently sang this song for me while she
was carding or quilting in front of the fire. It was one of her favorite songs. She
never seemed to question the appropriateness of singing it to a child. I always
asked for it because I liked the story and because I enjoyed the way her clear
soprano rose on the words, "Just spare, oh, spare me."

Though I have not seen a version of this song reported from England, I feel
that it is of English origin. Certainly the language is not American. The few versions reported from elsewhere in the United States vary only slightly from the one
printed here.

Sung by Jessie Ann Chennault Smith, Blossom, Texas, 1938.

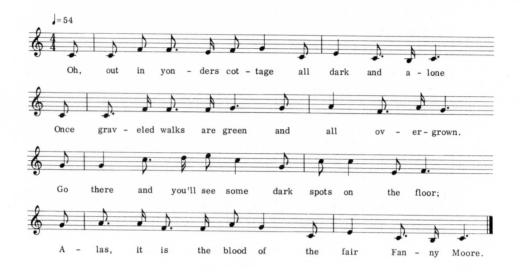

Oh, out in yonders cottage all dark and alone
Once graveled walks are green and all overgrown.
Go there and you'll see some dark spots on the floor;
Alas, it is the blood of the fair Fanny Moore.

When Fanny was blooming two lovers there came;
One offered his riches and he offered his fame;
His fame and his riches both failed to allure
The fond burning bosom of the fair Fanny Moore.

The next was young Edward, a man of low degree;
He offered his heart, enraptured was he,
And straightway to the altar he quickly did secure
The heart and the hand of the fair Fanny Moore.

When Fanny was sitting in her cottage one day—
Business had called her fond husband away—
Young Randall went out there, he opened the door
And clasped to his bosom the fair Fanny Moore.

"Oh, Randall, oh, Randall, oh, Randall," she cried,
"Just spare, oh, spare me," she wrung her hands and cried.
"Oh, Fanny, lovely Fanny, go to your land of rest,"
And he plunged a dagger through her snowy white breast.

While Fanny was bleeding, in her bloodstains she died,
Young Randall was taken and straightway was tried,
And hanged upon the willow by the side of the door
For shedding the blood of the fair Fanny Moore.

Young Edward, the shepherd, went distracted and wild;
He roamed awhile on his own native sod;
At last he was taken from his own cottage door
And laid by the side of the fair Fanny Moore.

BROTHER GREEN

This Union song has been reported from several southern states. Singers are apparently willing to overlook the Yankee setting for sentiments that might belong to North or South or border states between.

Sung by Mrs. Lee Kelly and her sister, Livingston, Texas, 1938.

Oh, Brother Green, do come to me,
For I am shot and bleeding;
The southern foe has laid me low,
On this cold ground to suffer.

Stay, Brother, stay and lay me away
And write my wife a letter;
Tell her that I'm prepared to die
And hope we'll meet in heaven.

Oh, Sister Nancy, do not weep
For the loss of your dear brother,
For he's gone home with Christ to dwell,
To see his blessed mother.

Two brothers yet I can't forget,
They're fighting for the Union,

And one dear wife—I'd give my life
To put down this rebellion.
And two little babes, I love them well,
Oh, could I once more see them,
I'd bid them all a sad farewell
Till we might meet in heaven.

Oh, Mary, you must treat them well,
And bring them up for heaven;
Teach them to love and serve the Lord
And then they'll be respected.

Oh, father, you have suffered long
And prayed for my salvation,
But now I'll be to home at last—
Farewell, farewell, temptation.

I WAS STANDING ON PICKETS

A poignant love song popular during the Civil War. The sentiments it expresses are universal enough for it to have come from that war or any other.

Sung by Rod Drake, Silsbee, Texas, 1952. There is considerable rhythmic flexibility.

"I was standing on pickets
One cold snowy day,
When I saw your old dead cheeks,
It was faded away."

Refrain:
   "Won't you let me go with you,
   It grieves my heart so;
   Won't you let me go with you?"
   "Oh, no, my love, no.

"Your waists are so slender,
Your fingers are too small,

And your face is too delicate
To face the cannon ball."

"Well, I know my waists are slender,
My fingers they are small,
But I don't think I'd tremble
To face the cannon ball."
   (*Refrain*)

"I would go before the captain,
Git down on my knees,
And ten thousand go 'gainst you
I'd give to you relief."
   (*Refrain*)

JESSE JAMES

When I was a child Jesse James was my greatest hero. My grandmother, whose maiden name was Alice James, was growing up in the vicinity of Camden, Arkansas, when the James brothers were at the height of their activity, and believed she was related to them. Jesse and Frank James, she said, came to her home to hide out from the law, and she was full of stories about how they had protected the helpless against the Yankees and how they had robbed the rich to give to the poor. Her own brother's sons were named Jesse and Frank in honor of the James boys. These cousins were frequently at our home, and the stories were told over and over and the song was sung again and again.

I was so filled with hero-worship that when one of my teachers called Jesse James a highway robber and thief in class one day, I stood up to protest and finally marched out of the schoolroom in anger. I might add that most of the other children in school were also of my opinion.

The Jesse James ballad came up for discussion and singing almost every time I went on recording trips. I have discovered several versions and half a dozen tunes.

Sung by May Kennedy McCord, Springfield, Missouri, 1939. The chords are from the singer's guitar accompaniment. There is variation in tempo.

Jesse James he was a man
Who was known throughout the land,
For Jesse he was bold and bad and brave;
But the dirty little coward
That murdered Mister Howard
Went and laid poor Jesse in his grave.

It was on a Friday night,
The moon was shining bright,
Robert Ford had been hiding in a cave;
He did eat of Jesse's bread
And he slept in Jesse's bed,
But he went and laid poor Jesse in his grave.

Refrain:
Jesse had a wife to mourn him all her life,
The children they were brave;

But the dirty little coward
That murdered Mister Howard
Went and laid poor Jesse in his grave.

It was Jesse's brother Frank
That robbed the Gallatin bank
And carried the money from the town;
It was in that very place
That they held a mighty race
And shot Captain Sheeks to the ground.
(Refrain)

Then they went to the station
Not very far from there,
And there Frank and Jesse did the same,
And the agent on his knees
Delivered up the keys
To the outlaws Frank and Jesse James.
(Refrain)

How the people held their breath
When they heard of Jesse's death
And wondered how he ever come to die;
But it was the sneaking coward,
The dirty Robert Ford
That shot Jesse James on the sly.
  (*Refrain*)

Jesse went to rest
With his hands upon his breast,
The devil he will look him in the face;
He was born one stormy day
In the County of old Clay
And came from a solitary race.
  (*Refrain*)

COLE YOUNGER

Sung by Rod Drake and his daughter, Mrs. Annie Mae Tousha, Silsbee, Texas, 1952.

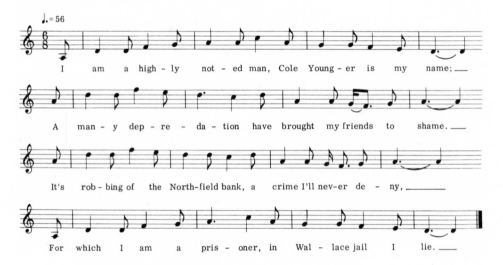

I am a highly noted man, Cole Younger is my name;
A many depredation have brought my friends to shame.
It's robbing of the Northfield bank, a crime I'll never deny,
For which I am a prisoner, in Wallace jail I lie.

The next thing took me on surprise, it was the U P train;
The dead had fought the bloody hand, brought tears unto my eyes,
The engineer and fireman killed, conductor came to die,
The tender bodies lay moulding there beneath Nebraska skies.

From out of my bold robbery a story I will tell
Of a California miner with whom I used to dwell.
I robbed him of his money and bid him go his way,
And that's a deed I shall regret until my dying day.

We got on our ponies and northward we did ride
All through that godforsaken country commencing with an O,

[*Line 3 missing.*]
A-fighting those anti-guerrilla boys until the day we died.

We got on our ponies and westward we did ride
While there all on the prairies the James boys we did meet
With guns and our revolvers we sit down for to play,
A-drinking a lot of good whiskey, boys, to pass the time away.

We got on our ponies and eastward we did ride;
I had my eye on Stoner's bank when Brother Bob did say,
[Third line missing]
"Cole, if you undertake that job you'll always curse the day."

We got off our ponies, into this bank did go,
While there all on the counter we dealt our fatal blow,
Saying, "Hand me out your money and don't make long delay,
For I am one of those Younger boys—I spare no time to pray."

THE BOSTON BURGLAR

An Americanized version of "Botany Bay," an English broadside, "The Boston
Burglar" is quite different in tone from the usual "bad man" ballads—probably
because the leading character is not identified with an outlaw whom tradition has
crowned with a halo.

Sung by Mrs. C. H. Burke, Silsbee, Texas, 1938. There is considerable variation
in tempo and flexibility in rhythm.

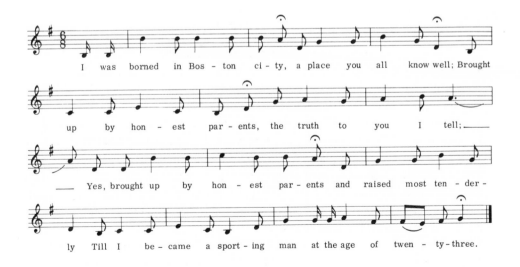

I was borned in Bos-ton ci-ty, a place you all know well; Brought
up by hon-est par-ents, the truth to you I tell;____
____ Yes, brought up by hon-est par-ents and raised most ten-der-
ly Till I be-came a sport-ing man at the age of twen-ty-three.

I was borned in Boston city, a place you all know well;
Brought up by honest parents, the truth to you I tell;
Yes, brought up by honest parents and raised most tenderly
Till I became a sporting man at the age of twenty-three.

And then my past was taken and I was sent to jail;
My parents tried to bail me out but it was of no avail.
The jurymen found me guilty, the clerk he wrote it down,
The judge pronounced my sentence to go to Sheriff's town.

I saw my aged father a-standing at the bar;
Likewise my aged mother a-pulling out her hair;
Yes, pulling out those old gray locks, the tears came rolling down,
Saying, "My son, what have you done, they sent you to Sheriff's town."

They put me on board of an eastbound train one cold December day,
And every station I passed through I heard those people say,
"There goes that Boston burglar, with iron chains bound down,
For some crime or other he's bound to Sheriff's town."

There's a girl in Boston city, and a girl that I love well,
And if ever I get my liberty alone with her I'll dwell;
Yes, if ever I get my liberty, bad company I'll shun,
Likewise my smoking and gambling and also drinking rum.

Come all young men who have your liberty, pray keep it if you can;
And don't go around those towns at night and break the laws of man.
For if you do you sure will be where the world will frown on you,
And you'll be serving your twenty-one years in the penitentiary.

THE TWO ORPHANS

When Lemuel Jeffus sang this song for me I asked him if the story had grown out of a real fire. He did not know of the Brooklyn Theater fire, and had but the vaguest notions what or where Brooklyn was. He thought, however, that the "two orphans" were guilty of setting fire to the theater.

From the *New York Times* I learned the full story of the fire at the Brooklyn Theater on the night of December 5, 1876, which broke out just as the curtain went up for the last act of the play *The Two Orphans*. The theater was crowded with twelve hundred persons; in spite of attempts by the actors to calm the crowd there was a stampede which blocked the exits and piled people together to suffocate and burn. More than 350 persons perished, among them some members of the cast. A mass burial was held for unidentified victims in Greenwood Cemetery, with Henry Ward Beecher as one of the speakers. There were also services at the Little Church Around the Corner for two of the actors—Claude Burroughs and Henry Murdock.

This service was attended by such celebrities as Edwin Booth, Dion Boucicault, and Sarah Orne Jewett.

A broadside account of the disaster was written by P. J. Downey and published by A. W. Auner of Philadelphia. It was to be sung to the tune of "Over the Hills to the Poor House." The song recorded here is a variant of that broadside, with minor changes in the words and a completely different tune.

Sung by Lemuel Jeffus, Lovelady, Texas, 1939.

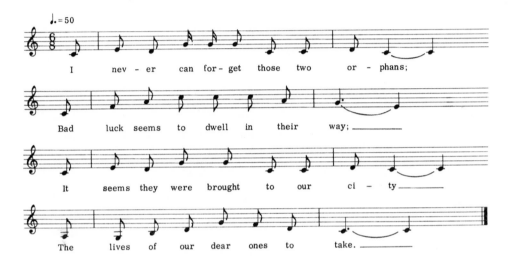

I never can forget those two orphans;
Bad luck seems to dwell in their way;
It seems they were brought to our city
The lives of our dear ones to take.

The doors were opened at seven,
And the curtains were rolled up at eight,
And those that were seated were happy;
Outside they were mad that were late.

It's hark, do you hear the cry fire?
How dismal those bells they do sound;
'Tis Brooklyn's Theater that's burning—
Alas, burning down to the ground.

The mothers were weeping and crying
For the sons who had been out all night;
They prayed that their souls would meet in heaven
Among the innocent and bright.

Next morning among those black ruins,
Oh, God, what a sight met our eyes;

The dead they were lying in all shapes;
Some of them you could not recognize.

I never can forget those two orphans;
Bad luck seems to dwell in their way;
It seems they were brought to our city
The lives of our dear ones to take.

THE GROG SHOP DOOR

Sung by Rod Drake, Silsbee, Texas, 1952.

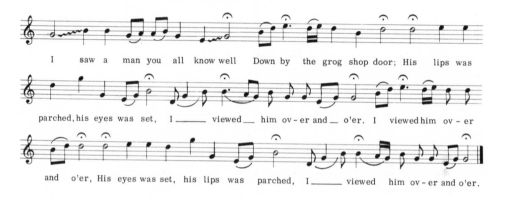

The singer breaks the regularity of the quarter note pulse (♩ =66) to emphasize important syllables, indicated here by a fermata (⌒).

I saw a man you all know well
Down by the grog shop door;
His lips was parched, his eyes was set,
I viewed him over and o'er.
I viewed him over and o'er,
His eyes was set, his lips was parched,
I viewed him over and o'er.

His aged sire stood by his side,
And to him faltering said,
"Father, mother sick at home,
And sister crying for bread,
And sister crying for bread,

Father, mother sick at home,
And sister crying for bread."

He got up, staggered to the door,
As he'd ofttime done before,
And to the landlord faltering said,
"Please give me one glass more,
Please give me one glass more,"
And to the landlord faltering said,
"Please give me one glass more."

Oh, that prehaps he passed away,
No wife, no child was there;
He drank while wife and children starved,
And ruined his poor soul.

THE ROVING GAMBLER

Negroes on the chain gang in Lamar County talked and sang a great deal about Dallas, "Big D," the nearest large city. Among their songs were "The Midnight Special," with the stanza

> If you ever go to Dallas,
> You better do right;
> You better not gamble
> And you better not fight.

and "The Deep Ellum Blues," from which I remember

> When you go to Dallas,
> Keep yo' money in yo' shoes,
> 'cause them Deep Ellum women
> Got them Deep Ellum Blues.

It was only natural for them to change the locale of "The Roving Gambler" to Dallas, as in the version presented here.

Apparently of Irish origin, this song has taken many forms in its wandering in the Old World and New. A version called "The Roving Journeyman," taken down from oral circulation in England, has most of the elements of the song printed here. Two stanzas illustrate the similarity:

> Young Jack he was a journeyman
> That roved from town to town,
> And when he'd done a job of work,
> He lightly sat him down.
> With his kit upon his shoulder, and
> A grafting knife in hand,
> He roved the country round about,
> A merry journeyman.
>
> And when he came to Exeter,
> The maidens leaped for joy;
> Said one and all, both short and tall,
> Here comes a gallant boy.
> The lady dropped her needle, and
> The maid her frying-pan,
> Each plainly told her mother that
> She loved the journeyman.

Sung by William A. Owens.

I am a rov - ing gam - bler, I rove from town to town;

Wher - ev - er I get a lit - tle bet I lay my mon - ey down.

I am a roving gambler,
I rove from town to town;
Wherever I get a little bet
I lay my money down.

I roved all down to Dallas,
All down to Dallas town—
There I got a little bet
And I laid my money down.

I had not been in Dallas
For many more weeks than three
When I fell in love with a Dallas girl
And she fell in love with me.

She asked me in her parlor,
She cooled me with her fan,

She whispered low in her mother's ear,
"I love this gambling man."

"Oh, daughter, oh, dear daughter,
How can you treat me so
To leave your dear old mother
And with this gambler go?"

"Oh, mother dear, I love you,
You know I love you well,
But the love I have for this gambling man
No human tongue can tell.

"Oh, mother dear, oh, mother,
I'll tell you if I can,
If you ever see me coming home again
It'll be with that gambling man."

ANGLO-AMERICAN LOVE SONGS

BALLADS OFTEN TELL stories of love unrequited. Love songs, as often, recite the sorrow, the moan, of the lover whose love is not returned. A happy love song is as rare as a happy ballad. The manner of the two was the same, and the routes traveled. Ballads made up in America, like those brought from Britain, often have identifiable persons, places, or incidents. Love songs rarely do. For instance, when "lovely Mary" is addressed there is no way to tell which Mary is meant. Identification of British elements in American survivals has to depend on internal evidence, and that is often not reliable. For example, the use of thyme as a symbol of virginity is British, not American, but willow is a symbol of sorrow in both. "Chickens A-Crowing on Sourwood Mountain" and "On Top of Old Smoky" are undeniably American. So are the art songs that have moved into the oral tradition.

"The Bright Mohawk Valley" is among the most widely traveled. Published as sheet music in the middle of the nineteenth century, it became popular with parlor performers and blackface minstrels alike. It spread west with the minstrel shows among people who had never heard of the Mohawk Valley in New York State. That association meaningless, singers changed the name to "The Red River Valley," likely the Red River of the South, though any one of the several Red Rivers could have served. In the version printed here it has been localized to Sherman, Texas, on that Red River and called "The Bright Sherman Valley."

Sentimental love songs flourished in America in the latter half of the nineteenth century, many of them circulated in sheet music, many of them the work of local composers. The death or impending death of a lover was a popular theme. The lyrics ran to the "you," "true," "blue" pattern, and the melodies were unsophisticated. Hardly romantic is the opening line of one: "Will you marry me, Ethel?" Leon said.

Such love songs were popular in rural America through the Great Depression and often appeared on the five-cent phonograph records sold in dime stores. A few of those included in this chapter are likely to survive. The others will still reflect an interesting period in the history of American folk song.

THE SAILOR BOY

Apparently British in origin—it has been reported from both England and Ireland—this song has had widespread popularity in America. I have found it on several occasions in East Texas, but always as a fragment. In a fuller version the sailor's body is washed ashore and the maid views it. Six weeks later she is dead of grief, having left the request, "Go dig my grave both wide and deep." In some versions the last stanza is the same as that of "The Butcher's Boy."

Sailor's trade is a dreary life,
It robs poor girls of their heart's delight;
Causes them to weep and mourn
The loss of a true love never to return.

Oh, brown be the color of my true love's hair,
His cheeks is like some lily fair;
When he returns it'll bring me joy,
For none can I love but my sweet sailor boy.

She met three ships all come from Spain,
All heavy loaded as they could swim;
She hailed each captain as they passed by
And there she inquired for her sweet sailor boy.

"Captain, captain, tell me true,
Does sweet Willie sail with you?"
"No, no, he's not here;
He got drowned in the gulf, my dear."

She wrung her hands and she tore her hair
Like someone in deep despair.
"If ever he returns it'll bring me joy,
For none can I love but my sweet sailor boy."

NORA DARLING

The song of the emigrant ready to set out from Europe to America appears in various languages in ballad literature. The Germans who left for Texas around 1848 sailed with the tune and words of "Muss i denn" in their ears, and were greeted at the wharf in Galveston by a German band playing the same song. It is no wonder that this song of a young man pleading with his sweetheart to go to the New World with him should still be among the most popular with Texas Germans today. Louisiana French sing essentially the same theme in "Le Breton." And the Irish gave us "Nora Darling," which my father's family apparently brought to Texas from Indiana.

Sung by William A. Owens.

"I am going far away, Nora darling,
The ship is at anchor in the bay;
And before tomorrow's sun
You will hear the signal gun,
So be ready and it'll take us far away."

"I'd go with you there, Barney darling,
But I've often told you the reason why;
It would break my mother's heart
If from her I had to part
And go roaming with you Barney McCoy."

"Then come with me there, Nora darling,
Bid all your friends in Ireland goodbye;
For 'tis happy you will be
In the dear land of the free
And a-roaming with your Barney McCoy."

"I will go with you then, Barney darling,
Bid all my friends in Ireland goodbye,
For it would break my heart in two
If I had to part from you,
So I'll go roaming with Barney McCoy."

THE IRISH GIRL

Sung by Daniel Jeffus, Lovelady, Texas, 1939. The chords are from the singer's guitar accompaniment.

As I walked out one morn-ing, Down by the riv-er side; My eyes were cast a-round me, And an I-rish girl I spied.

As I walked out one morning,
Down by the river side,
My eyes were cast around me,
And an Irish girl I spied.

So red and rosy were her cheeks,
And so curly was her hair,
And so costly was her jewelry
That Irish girl did wear.

The tears came trickling down her cheeks,
And she began to cry,
Said, "My true love's gone to Ireland
And highly forsaken am I."

I wish I was in Ireland,
Sitting in a chair,
Within my hand a glass of wine
And my true love by my side.

I'd call for candy kisses,
And pay them as I go,
I'd sail across the ocean,
Let the winds blow high or low.

Love, oh, love, it's a killing thing,
Did you ever feel the pain?
How hard it is to love anyone,
And never be loved again.

FOND AFFECTION

The lure of free land in the Indian Territory drew a number of my relatives away from Pin Hook and to the vicinity of what is now Purcell, Oklahoma. In the years that passed there was considerable visiting back and forth, with the usual swapping of songs. "Fond Affection" is one of the songs brought to us by our Oklahoma cousins. How it came to them I have never known; it has seldom been reported from other parts of the United States.

Sung by Miss Willie Haigood, Purcell, Oklahoma, 1939.

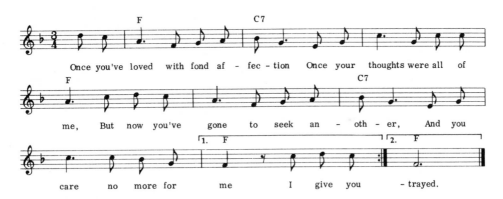

Once you've loved with fond affection
Once your thoughts were all of me,
But now you've gone to seek another,
And you care no more for me.

I give you back your ring and letters,
And the picture I have loved so well,

And henceforth we will meet as strangers,
But I can never say farewell.

The only things that I could wish for,
Are my coffin, shroud, and grave,
And when I'm dead don't weep o'er me,
Or kiss the lips you once betrayed.

BURY ME BENEATH THE WILLOW

This song, known in almost every Texas community, is often sung as a duet by soprano and alto harmonizing in thirds. No doubt it is an old song, though I have not been successful in tracing its history. The willow is the traditional symbol of sorrow.

Sung by Miss Willie Haigood and Mrs. Myrtle Woodward, Purcell, Oklahoma, 1939.

Tomorrow is our wedding day,
God only knows where he may be;
He's gone to seek another bride,
And now he cares no more for me.

Refrain:
Oh, bury me beneath the willow,
Beneath the weeping willow tree,
And when he knows where I lie
sleeping
Perhaps he will then think of me.

My heart is broken, I'm in sorrow,
Weeping for the one I love,
For I know I ne'er shall see him
Till we meet in heaven above.
          (*Refrain*)

They told me that he did not love me,
How could I think he'd be untrue,
Until an angel whispered to me,
"He will prove untrue to you."
          (*Refrain*)

THE BIRMINGHAM JAIL

On a farm next to the one I grew up on lived a family by the name of White. Mrs. White, whose other name I cannot remember, had a high soprano that carried across fields and woods with the shrillness of a steam whistle. Day after day she worked in the cotton fields with her husband and two sons, doing work too heavy for the average woman, but doing it uncomplainingly. In the late afternoon, when the sun was about an hour high, she would start singing, usually "The Birmingham Jail." Over and over again she would sing the sad words, allowing her voice to reach a high tremolo at least twice during each stanza. Often she would still be singing the song when sunset came. Working on our side of the fence, we could follow the course of her footsteps across the fields and up to her house, as she continued the song until she disappeared.

In January, 1945, I was on an LST in a convoy going up for the invasion of Luzon. Much of the voyage was through Japanese-controlled waters and the convoy was subject to frequent Kamikaze attacks. Every afternoon just before vespers there was a period of recorded music over the public address system. Every afternoon I sat on the deck and heard the strains of "The Birmingham Jail" float out over the waters of the Sulu and China seas. Our situation then seemed unreal. For me the reality was the memory of Mrs. White singing as she cut across the cotton rows.

This song has been thoroughly absorbed into the American mind and now belongs as much to nightclub performers as to the lonesome singers down where the Birmingham jail has a special significance.

Sung by William A. Owens.

Down in the valley,
The valley so low,
Late in the evening
I heard a train blow;
I heard a train blow, love,
Heard a train blow,
Late in the evening
I heard a train blow.

Bird in the cage, love,
Swinging so high;
Kiss me once, darling,
Tell me goodbye.

Bird in the cage, love,
Swinging so low;
Kiss me once, darling,
Then I must go.

Roses love sunshine,
Violets love dew,
Angels in heaven
Know I love you.
Write me a letter,
Send it by mail,
Send it in care of
The Birmingham Jail.

MY BLUE-EYED BOY

Sung by Miss Willie Haigood, Purcell, Oklahoma, 1939.

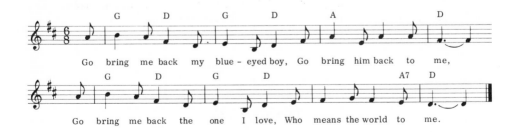

Go bring me back my blue-eyed boy,
Go bring him back to me,
Go bring me back the one I love,
Who means the world to me.

I don't know why I love him,
He never cared for me;
He can seek this wide world over,
He'll find no girl like me.

There's changes in the ocean,
There's changes in the sea,
There's changes in the one I love,
There'll be no change in me.

There's changes in the seasons,
There's changes in the time,
There's changes in the poor boy's heart,
There'll be no change in mine.

THEY SAY IT IS SINFUL TO FLIRT

Sung by Miss Willie Haigood, Purcell, Oklahoma, 1939.

They say it is sin-ful to flirt,___ They say his heart is made of stone,___
So I will speak to him kind - ly And leave the poor boy___ a - lone. ___

They say it is sinful to flirt,
They say his heart is made of stone,
So I will speak to him kindly
And leave the poor boy alone.

They say he is only a boy,
I'm sure he's much older than me,
And if they'd leave us alone
I'm sure much happier we'd be.

I remember the night when he said,
"I love you more dearly than life."
He called me his darling, his pet,
And asked me to be his dear wife.

"Oh, darling," I said with a smile,
"I'm sure I will have to say no."
He took a rose from my hair,
And said, "Goodbye, I must go."

Next morning the dear boy was found
Drowned in the pond by the mill;
Pressed close to his heart was the rose
That he had took from my hair.

"Oh, Willie, my darling, come back,
I'll always be loving and true;
Oh, Willie, my darling come back,
I'll ever be faithful to you."

TOO LATE

Sung by Miss Mayme Finch, Detroit, Texas, 1941.

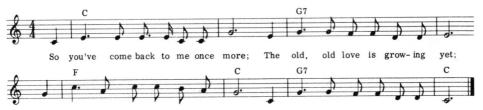

So you've come back to me once more; The old, old love is grow-ing yet;

You've tried through all these ma-ny years, You've tried though vain-ly to for - get.

So you've come back to me once more;
The old, old love is growing yet;
You've tried through all these many years,
You've tried though vainly to forget.

So you've come back to me once more,
Since time at last has made you free,
To ask again of me the heart
Whose early ties are bound in thee.

Come near and let me see your face,
Your chestnut hair is tinged with snow,
Yet still it is the same old face
I loved so many years ago;

The same that on that summer's eve
Bent over me and kissed my brow—
Those happy, happy hours of love,
Ah, well, they are all over now.

Oh, no, you cannot take my hand,
God ne'er gives us back our youth;
The gulf between can ne'er be spanned,
Our paths must lie apart in sooth.

Forgive—you do not speak the word;
You never meant to do me wrong.
God sent this anguish to my heart
To teach me to be brave and strong.

A woman's soul, a woman's tongue
Must know and speak the truth;
You left me when my heart was sore—
No voice can e'er restore our youth.

Farewell, I think I love you yet
As friend loves friend—God bless you, dear,
And guide you through life's darkest ways
To where the skies are always clear.

LORENE

In the spring of 1941 I went to see Mayme Finch at her home on the highway between Detroit and Clarksville in Texas. A cripple all her life, she had turned to the guitar and songs for her own entertainment. In talking to me about picking the guitar she said, "I jest pick it straight; I don't know none of them crooked chords." She actually could manage only three chords—but these were enough to accompany most of the songs she sang. I had known "Lorene" a long time as a fiddle tune, but the first and only time I found all the words to it was when Mayme Finch sang it for me. The tune has long been a favorite with country fiddlers.

Sung by Miss Mayme Finch, Detroit, Texas, 1941.

The bright light was shining in heaven,
The stars were all twinkly and blue;
The soft bonnie breeze of the twilight
Reminds me, my dear one, of you.
Last night as we parted in sorrow
With heavy hearts hasting away,
You promised, my darling, to meet me
To give me your answer today.

Refrain:
Give me your answer, Lorene, today;
Say you'll be mine, love,
Don't turn away.
You are my angel, my star, my queen;
Give me your answer
Today, sweet Lorene.

They say that you'll go to some city,
Where be loved ones you're seeking to find;
With the rich and the gay you will mingle
And the friends you are leaving behind.
You know that you promised me, darling,
That you would soon make my life joy;
Come look in my eyes for this moment
And give me your answer today.
         (*Refrain*)

ON TOP OF OLD SMOKY

No collection of Texas folk songs would be complete without "On Top of Old Smoky." Originating in the southern mountains, it followed the migration of the folk to Texas, where it has become a part of the song store of almost every fiddler and guitar-picker. The stanzas are interchanged with those from "Rye Whiskey," "Some Say I Drink Whiskey," and "The Rebel Soldier." All of these are no doubt descended from the British song, "The Unconstant Lover."

On top of old Smoky,
All covered with snow,
I lost my true lover,
By courting too slow.

Courting's a pleasure,
Parting is grief,
And a false-hearted lover
Is worse than a thief.

It's raining, it's hailing;
The moon gives no light;
Your horses cain't travel
This dark lonesome night.

Put up your horses
And feed them some hay;
Come sit down beside me
As long as you stay.

My horses ain't hungry;
They won't eat your hay;
So farewell, my darling,
I'll feed on the way.

I'm going to Texas;
I'll tell you my mind;
I'm going to marry
And leave you behind.

THE BRIGHT SHERMAN VALLEY

No folk song has been more widely sung by all types of Americans than "Red River Valley"; no other has been claimed by so many regions. Residents of the valley of the Red River of the North call it their own. Residents of the Red River Valley of the South are just as certain it is a song about their river. Many Texans have told me it was "made up" at Sherman, Texas.

The truth is that the song was originally written about the Mohawk Valley of New York and called "In the Bright Mohawk Valley." It was composed and published as sheet music in the middle of the nineteenth century, and thus has been in oral circulation more than a hundred years. Though the title has changed, both words and music have, strangely enough, remained remarkably faithful to the original.

In my early associations this was a "lonesome song." Negroes on chain gangs, in the bottomland cotton fields—or wherever they were set to work—sang it in a slow soft murmur as they labored. Whites sang it too, picking out the tune when they could on guitar or banjo. It formed a background for our lives and work even more realistically than it did for the Joads in the motion picture version of *The Grapes of Wrath*.

Sung by Daniel Jeffus, Lovelady, Texas, 1939.

From this valley they tell me you're leaving;
I will miss your bright eyes and sweet smile,
For you take with you all of the sunshine
That has lightened my path for awhile.
Do you think of the home you are leaving,
Of the parents so kind and so true?
Do you think of the fond heart you're breaking,
Of the girl who has loved you so true?

Refrain:
> Just consider a while ere you leave me;
> Do not hasten to bid me adieu;
> Just remember the bright Sherman valley
> And the girl who has loved you so true.

> For a long time I've waited, my darling,
> For the sweet words you never would say,
> And at last my fond heart now is breaking,
> For they tell me you're going away.
> When you go from the scenes of this valley,
> And they tell me your journey is through,
> Just remember the bright Sherman valley
> And the girl who has loved you so true.
> *(Refrain)*

GOODBYE, LITTLE BONNIE BLUE EYES

I first heard "Goodbye, Little Bonnie Blue Eyes" at the Texas Centennial when May Kennedy McCord of Springfield, Missouri, sang it on one of the programs of the National Folk Festival. Since then I have found it in the Big Thicket under the same title, and in the Brush Country as "Goodbye, Little Birdie, Goodbye." Apparently of southern mountain origin, the song has become a favorite on hillbilly radio programs and has spread throughout the Southwest. The stanza form and melody lend themselves to easy improvisation; as a result there are almost as many variations in the stanzas as there are singers of the song. It was easily parodied, as the following refrain shows:

> Goodbye, little bonnie blue eyes,
> Goodbye, little bonnie blue eyes,
> You told me you loved me
> But you told me a lie,
> Goodbye, little bonnie blue eyes.

It was as easily turned to protest and became one of the popular protest songs during the Great Depression, especially among labor organizers in the South.

Sung by May Kennedy McCord, Springfield, Missouri, 1939. The chords are from the singer's guitar accompaniment.

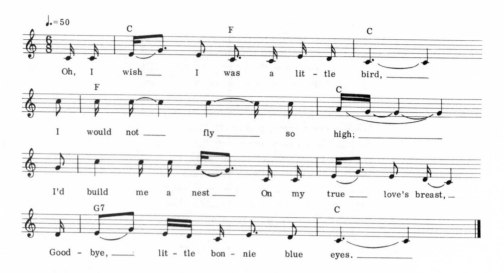

Oh, I wish I was a little bird,
I would not fly so high;
I'd build me a nest
On my true love's breast,
Goodbye, little bonnie blue eyes.

Refrain:

    Goodbye, little bonnie blue eyes,
    Goodbye, little bonnie blue eyes,
    I'll see you again,
    But God knows when,
    Goodbye, little bonnie blue eyes.

I'm going on the ocean blue,
Where the mountains reach the sky,
On the ocean blue
I'll be thinking about you,
Goodbye, little bonnie blue eyes.
    (Refrain)

Oh, lay your hand in mine,
Oh, lay your hand in mine,
If you love me
Like I love you,
Honey, lay your hand in mine.
    (Refrain)

MY PRETTY LITTLE PINK

Sung by Mrs. Dan Williams of Washington, D.C., who learned it from her father in Rockdale, Texas.

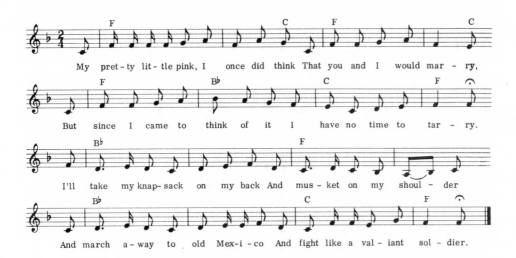

My pretty little pink, I once did think
That you and I would marry,
But since I came to think of it
I have no time to tarry.

I'll take my knapsack on my back
And musket on my shoulder
And march away to old Mexico
And fight like a valiant soldier.

Where coffee grows on whiteoak trees
And rivers flow with brandy,
And the rocks are painted all over with gold
And the girls are sweeter than candy.

JACK AND JOE

Sung by Miss Willie Haigood and Mrs. Myrtle Woodward, Purcell, Oklahoma, 1939.

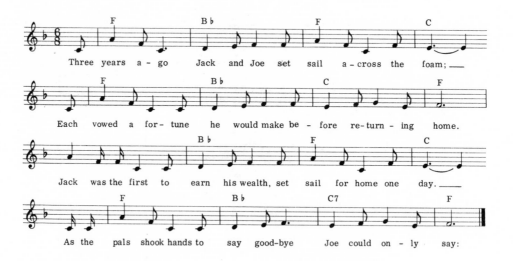

Three years ago Jack and Joe set sail across the foam;
Each vowed a fortune he would make before returning home.
Jack was the first to earn his wealth, set sail for home one day.
As the pals shook hands to say goodbye Joe could only say:

Refrain:
    "Give my love to Nellie, Jack, kiss her once for me;
    The sweetest girl in all the world I know you'll say 'tis she.
    Treat her kindly, Jack, old pal, and tell her I am well."
    His parting words were "Don't forget to give my love to Nell."

Three years had passed when Joe at last had earned his wealth for life;
Set sail for home across the foam to make sweet Nell his wife.
There he learned that Jack and Nell one year ago had wed;
It was then he spoke the first regret that he had ever said:
    (Refrain)

They chanced to meet upon the street. Joe said, "You selfish elf,
The next time I learn to love a girl I'll kiss her for myself;
But all is fair in love and war and you and Nell have wed—
I won't be angry, Jack, old pal," and thus again he said:
    (Refrain)

ANGLO-AMERICAN COMIC SONGS

HUMOR WAS SOMETIMES AN ELEMENT in British ballads brought to America—a major element in "The Farmer's Curst Wife" and "Our Goodman." At times it was general, as in the use of nonsense rhymes in songs like "Rolly Troodum" and nonsense statements like those in "Noddingham Town." At times it was specific, especially in the songs that recount conflicts between husbands and wives. In this chapter the male-female battle, whether imported from Britain or improvised on the frontier, rolls on in a half-dozen or more songs. It ranges from the light and rollicking laughter of "I Wish to My Lord I Was Single Again" to the sick sad wail of "Gee, I Wish I Was a Single Girl Again." There may be exaggeration on the surface. Underneath, there is a ring of truth.

Exaggeration, whether imported or not, was a device immediately popular on the frontier, where living conditions were so extreme, local characters so individualistic, that further exaggeration hardly seemed possible. Exaggeration became the biggest lie a liar could tell, and there was competition to determine the biggest whether in song or story. Such imagined heroes as Paul Bunyan became a part of frontier lore. So did real heroes like Daniel Boone and Davy Crockett, both of whom lent themselves willingly to the exaggeration of their deeds—as in "Pompey Smash and Davy Crockett," wherein the fight between the imaginary Davy Crockett and the imaginary Pompey became a part of blackface minstrelsy.

Blackface minstrels, themselves a creation of the American frontier, borrowed comic songs from the people when they could, improvised when they could not. They moved characters and situations from one song to another to suit their fancy or to provoke greater laughter from their portrayals of southern Negro life. The composition of "I Wish I Was in Dixie Land," more commonly called "Dixie," is to the point. Dan Emmett took a name in common usage for the Southland, "Dixie," and added to it from at least one other source, the ballad "Will the Weaver." In the ballad Will the Weaver, also called "the false deceiver," is caught by another man in bed with that man's wife. Will the Weaver is discovered hiding in the chimney, pulled down with a pole, and beaten blacker than a chimney sweeper. Emmett's borrowing appears in the second stanza:

> Old Missus marry Will-de weaber,
> Willium was a gay deceaber;
> Look away, look away, look away, Dixie Land!
> But when he put his arm around 'er,
> He smiled as fierce as a forty-pounder;
> Look away, look away, look away, Dixie Land!

A forty-pounder was a cannon almost big enough itself to be an exaggeration.

Rough, bawdy, or gently ironic, these songs traveled with the people and often made them laugh when they wanted to cry.

THE WIDOW OF McCARTY

Sung by Rod Drake, Silsbee, Texas, 1952. There is variation in the tempo and flexibility in rhythmic treatment of individual lines.

A-bout a week a-go to-day___ I tak-ened me a wife And ev-er since that day she's been the bur-den to my life; She's the wi-dow of Mc-Car-ty and Mc-Car-ty was her name,___ But for chang-ing it to Reil-ly, well, of course she's not to blame. Well, she speaks of him most ev-ery day_____ and to the neigh-bors say, "I wish that he'd be so-ber and be like him ev-ery way." But to boss of my own furn-i-ture I'll do the best I can;___ Mc-Car-ty was an an-gel but now she's got a man.

About a week ago today I takened me a wife
And ever since that day she's been the burden to my life;
She's the widow of McCarty and McCarty was her name,
But for changing it to Reilly, well, of course she's not to blame.

Well, she speaks of him most every day, and to the neighbors say,
"I wish that he'd be sober and be like him every way."
But to boss of my own furniture I'll do the best I can;
McCarty was an angel but now she's got a man.

Well, I'm going down to Grady's just on purpose to get tight,
And if I do come home agin there's going to be a fight;
I'll smash-up all the furniture a-standing by the room,
And I'll upset the cooking stove the first thing that I do.

And if I ever hear her mention McCarty's name agin,
I'll show her who's the best man, McCarty or me then;
Well, I'll learn her how to fly a kite and try to lead the band—
McCarty was an angel, but now she's got a man.

Well, she bite him, she scratch him, and she wouldn't let him be;
She fight him and she scratch him until he couldn't see;
Well, the fighting hadn't started till she got a different party,
And she might lick McCarty but, by gosh, she cain't lick me.

Well, she beat him with a broomstick every time the baby cried,
And she made him rock the cradle until the day he died;
And when he wouldn't stir himself and try to mend the clothes,
Well, the frying pan was all content to try and break his nose.

NODDINGHAM TOWN

Sung by Rod Drake, Silsbee, Texas, 1952. There is considerable rhythmic
flexibility.

I start-ed one day to fair Nod-ding-ham town, A - rid-ing a horse like a-
walk-ing be-fore With a lit-tle nig-ger drum-mer a - beat-ing a drum
With his heels in his pock-ets be - fore he could run.

I started one day to fair Noddingham town,
A-riding a horse like a-walking before
With a little nigger drummer a-beating a drum
With his heels in his pockets before he could run.

Well, the king and the queen and the company more,
A-riding a horse like a-walking before
With a little nigger drummer a-beating a drum
With his heels in his pockets before he could run.

I rode up to Mister Madison's gate
Inquiring the way for I knew not the place;
They was all so mad till they'd scarcely look around
To tell me the way to fair Noddingham Town.

Well, my mare she stood still and she throwed me in a ditch,
She bruised my shirt, she dirtied my skin;
With the saddle and stirrups I'll mount her again
And with my ten toes I'll ride over the plain.

It rained and it hailed and it snowed and it blowed.
Ten thousand around me, I set there alone;
I called for a bottle to drive sadness away—
I stifled in dust and it rained all that day.

I'll gear up my black horses, a-fishing I'll go,
Yes, I will, yes, I will whether or no;
My cart it turned over, my fish it did spill,
I'll sell them black horses, yes, damn 'em, I will.

IT WAS A YOUNG MAN

Sung by Rod Drake, Silsbee, Texas, 1952.

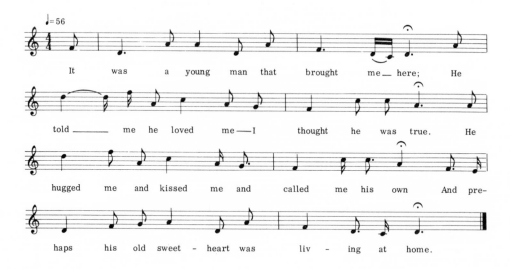

It was a young man that brought me— here;   He
told _____ me he loved me —I thought he was true.   He
hugged me and kissed me and called me his own   And prehaps his old sweet - heart was liv - ing at home.

It was a young man that brought me here;
He told me he loved me—I thought he was true.
He hugged me and kissed me and called me his own
And prehaps his old sweetheart was living at home.

Hard is the feature of a poor womankind;
They're always controlled, and they're always confined;
They're controlled by their parents until they're made wives,
And been slaves for their husbands the balance of their lives.

COME ALL YOU FAIR MAIDENS

Sung by Rod Drake, Silsbee, Texas, 1952.

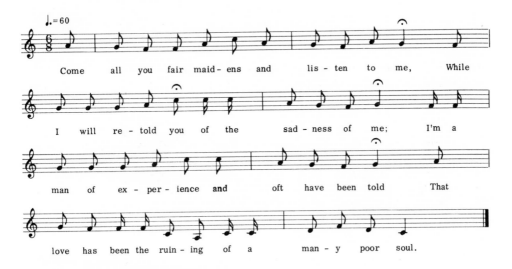

Come all you fair maidens and listen to me,
While I will retold you of the sadness of me;
I'm a man of experience and oft have been told
That love has been the ruining of a many poor soul.

Your young men do dress up, they'll think themselves smart,
While courtin' a many a smiling sweetheart;
They'll come dancing before you great favors to gain,
But come and take warning they're trouble and pain.

Oh, when you are married you're not your own man,
In roving this country you go in a band;
You've lost a sweet flower, the sweetest of life,
For selling your freedom to buy you a wife.

You cain't step aside to speak to a friend,
What they will embrace you saying, "Where have you been?"
They'll turn up their noses, look worst in bad news,
Boys, come and take warning their life to refuse.

But when you are single you are your own man,
Go when you git ready, return when you can;
Eat, drink, and be merry and do your own will,
Court any young lady and leave the same still.

Now fill up your glasses,
Drink health all around,
Here's luck to the poet where he may be found,
Likewise to the single I hope them no less.

DEAR JOHN

"Dear John" is a version of "Springfield Mountain," a quite different version from the "Joh-woh-wonny" version I knew when I was a child. The origin of the song can be found in an account by Josiah Gilber Holland (*History of Western Massachusetts*, 2:161-62):

On the 7th of August, 1761, occurred an event which has been celebrated in song. It is doubtful whether any piece of American doggerel has been so fortunate in the term of its perpetuation. It relates to the death of Timothy Merrick, from the bite of a rattlesnake, and has been added to and modified until the versions of it are numerous. The verses are said to have been written by a young woman to whom the unfortunate man was engaged to be married. . . .

By 1865 the song had lost its tragic character and humorous stanzas had been added. The last two stanzas of one of those comic versions illustrate the change:

Then Molly Bland, she squatted down,
And sucked the pizen from the wound;
But, oh! she had a rotten tewth;
The venim soon affected both.

Oh, then they were all spotted o'er
With all the colors the serpent wore;
They laid 'em both upon a bed,
And they swelled up and di-i-ed.

Sung by Rod Drake, Silsbee, Texas, 1952.

One Sunday morning poor John did go
Down in this meadow for to mow;
He had not more'n crossed the field,
For up jumped a blacksnake and bit him on the heel.
Tum a row row ridden um ridden um ray
Tum a row row ridden um ray.

His old father standing by
Viewed him through the shade of a whiteoak bough,
Picked up a blade to give it a swipe
Tum a row row ridden um ridden um ray
Tum a row row ridden um ridden um ray
Tum a row row ridden um ray.

"Dear Dad, dear Dad, go inform my girl,
For it's time to die and I know I shall."
Away went Dad and he told the news,
And here comes Ma without her shoes,
Tum a row row ridden um ridden um ray
Tum a row row ridden um ray.

"Dear John, dear John, why did you go
Down in this meadow for to mow?"
"Oh, Law', Ma, I thought you knowed
That Daddy's wheat had not been mowed."
Tum a row row ridden um ridden um ray
Tum a row row ridden um ray.

Dear John did die, to heaven did go,
Crying, "Cruel Ma, I thought you knowed."
Ride around now for to make his bow;
If he cain't git back he's there right now,
Tum a row row ridden um ridden um ray
Tum a row row ridden um ray.

BRYNIE O'LINN

Sung by Rod Drake, Silsbee, Texas, 1952.

Brynie O'Linn he had no britches to wear;
He taken a sheep skin and cut him out a pair,
With the wool side in and the flesh side out.
"Was a very funny pants," said Brynie O'Linn.
[*Snort*] doodle de dandy.

Brynie O'Linn he had but one horse to ride,
[Line 2 is lacking]
And his back broke in and his sides caved in.
And it's a very funny horse," said Brynie O'Linn.
[*Snort*] doodle de dandy.

COME ALL YOU MISSISSIPPI GIRLS

a. Sung by Rod Drake, Silsbee, Texas, 1952.

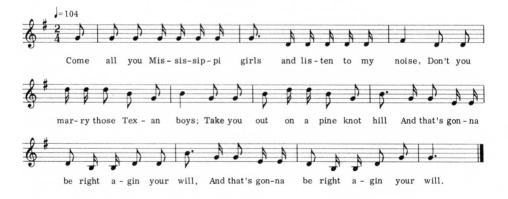

Come all you Mississippi girls and listen to my noise,
Don't you marry those Texan boys;
Take you out on a pine knot hill
And that's gonna be right agin your will,
And that's gonna be right agin your will.

Let me tell you how they dress,
An old black dyed shirt and that's the very best;
An old straw hat more brim than crown
And that's the way those Texans dress,
And that's the way those Texans dress.

When they go courting pick them up a chair
And the first word they say, "Daddy killed a deer."
[*Line 3 missing.*]
Johnny cake a-baking was a fine young man,
Johnny cake a-baking was a fine young man.

Have an old cow, milked her in a gourd,
Set it in the corner and cover it with a board;
Some gets a little and some gets none
And that's just the way those Texans run,
And that's just the way those Texans run.

They git hungry before they go to bed,
They build them up a fire high as one's head;
Rake back the ashes and blow off the coals
And all they call for is beef, boys beef,
And all they call for is beef, boys, beef.

b. Variation with essentially the same tune but different words; sung by Mark
Hathaway, Livingston, Texas, 1941.

Come all you Missouri girls and listen to my noise
And don't you marry them Texas boys,
Take you out on a sand flat hill
And that will be against your will,
And that will be against your will.

Way up yonder is a little hill,
And a way down yonder is a little field—
Gourds and pumpkins grows there fine,
Or anything else that'll grow on a vine,
Or anything else that'll grow on a vine.

Some take a liking to the hewed log walls
Without any windows in them a-tall,
Stick and place chimney and a battened door
And a clapboard roof and a puncheon floor,
And a clapboard roof and a puncheon floor.

When they go a-courting they take a chair,
And the first thing they say is "Daddy killed a deer,"
And the next thing they say when they set down,
"Lord God, johnny cake's cooking rather brown,
Lord God, johnny cake's cooking rather brown."

If they have a cow they milk her in a gourd,
Set it in a corner and cover it with a board;
Some gets a little and some gets none
And that is the way with a Tex-i-un,
And that is the way with a Tex-i-un.

If they get hungry before they go to bed
They build up a fire at the husband's head,
Rake away the ashes and roll in the dough,
And it's all they call for is "Dough, boys, dough,"
And all they call for is "Dough, boys, dough."

WENT OUT A-SPARKIN'

Sung by Maidy Kelly, Livingston, Texas, 1938. Each stanza has from one to three lines with the music of line one and then the two closing lines.

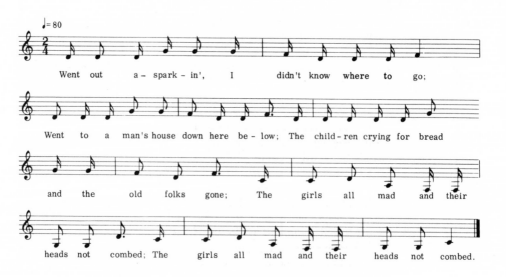

Went out a-sparkin', I didn't know where to go;
Went to a man's house down here below;
The children crying for bread and the old folks gone;
The girls all mad and their heads not combed;
The girls all mad and their heads not combed.

I sat and sparked till I got ashamed,
And every once in a while they'd ask me my name;
And every once in a while they'd ask me my name.

When they go to cook I'll tell you how they do;
They build up a fire as high as your head;
Scratch out the ashes and pile them on the bread;
Scratch out the ashes and pile them on the bread.

They called me to dinner and I thought for to eat;
The first thing I saw was a big chunk of meat
Cooked half done and tough as a maul,
An old ash cake baked bran and all;
An old ash cake baked bran and all.

One old knife and nary a fork;
I sawed for an hour and couldn't make a mark;
I sawed for an hour and couldn't make a mark.

Kept on sawing till I got it out of my plate.
One of the girls says, "You'd better wait."
Kept on sawing till I got it on the floor,
Up with my foot and kicked it out the door;
Up with my foot and kicked it out the door.

'Long come the old man with his double-barreled gun.
One of the girls says, "You'd better run."
Stood and fought him brave as a bear,
Tangled my fingers in the old man's hair;
Tangled my fingers in the old man's hair.

When you go to church I'll tell you what to wear,
An old cotton dress and that's the very best;
An old lint sack, grease all around,
An old leather bonnet with a hole in the crown;
An old leather bonnet with a hole in the crown.

HARD TIMES

Sung by Rod Drake, Silsbee, Texas, 1952.

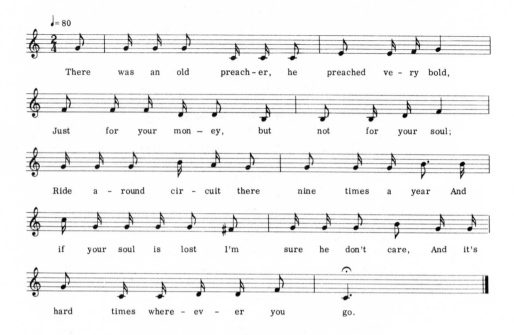

There was an old preacher, he preached very bold,
Just for your money but not for your soul;
Ride around circuit there nine times a year
And if your soul is lost I'm sure he don't care,
And it's hard times wherever you go.

There was an old miller a-joggin along,
Feeding his hogs on other people's corn,
Speak to the farmer and he'd speak very bold,
And if you don't watch him he'll take double toll,
And it's hard times wherever you go.

There was an old doctor I like to a forgot,
I believe to my soul he's the worst in the lot,
Promise to cure you for half you possess,
And when you are dead he'll sue you for the rest,
And it's hard times wherever I go.

Once I had Union and then I had peas,
Plenty of bacon and plenty of grease,
Plenty of powder and plenty of lead,
To bust into that little Confed,
And it's hard times wherever I go.

THE YOUNG MEN THEY'LL DRESS UP

Sung by Rod Drake, Silsbee, Texas, 1952.

The young men they'll dress up so neat and so fine,
A-courting of those pretty girls it is their desire;
They will court and they'll spy and they'll tell them the lie,
And they'll keep up all those pretty girls 'til they're ready for to die.

Well, away toward midnight those girls they will say,
"I'm grew mighty sleepy, boys, I wisht you would go 'way."
"Before I will go 'way I will sleep in the barn,
Before I will go 'way I will sleep in the barn."

They'll get up next morning and they'll stagger and they'll reel.
"God bless all those pretty girls, how sleepy I do feel—
If you ask me the way I will court none at all,
I live a single life and keep bachelors and all."

"Go home every night and partake of my rest,
No woman for to bawl and no children for to squall,
No woman for to bawl and no children to squall,
How happy is the young man that's got none at all."

NOT THE ONLY TURTLE IN THE TANK

Sung by Rod Drake, Silsbee, Texas, 1952.

When you think yourself an oyster and felicitate yourself,
On your standing and your balance in the bank,
Just remember there's another one just respectful as you,
And you're not the only turtle in the tank.

Refrain:

    So take your honors easily and don't git all swelled up,
    For your folks will find you're also but a blank,
    And the world will move without you and you never will be missed
    'Cause you're not the only turtle in the tank.

There's a self made man's a wonder and he'll tell you so himself,
For there's no one but him to really thank,
And his method is more simple and he'll try to make you think
That he is the only turtle in the tank.
    (*Refrain*)

OLD KINCAID

Sung by Rod Drake, Silsbee, Texas, 1952.

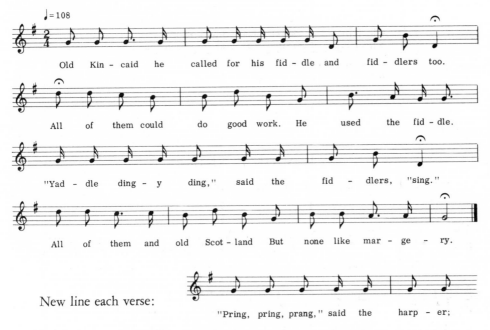

New line each verse:

Old Kincaid he called for his fiddle and fiddlers too.
All of them could do good work. He used the fiddle.
"Yaddle dingy ding," said the fiddlers, "sing."
All of them and old Scotland
But none like margery.

Old Kincaid he called for a harper too.
All of them could do good work. He used the harp.
"Pring, pring, prang," said the harper;
"Yaddle dingy ding," said the fiddlers, "sing."
All of them in old Scotland
But none like margery.

Old Kincaid he called for a barber, too.
All of them could do good work. He used the razor.
"Hold up your chin," said the barber;
"Pring, pring, prang," said the harper;
"Yaddle dingy ding," said the fiddlers, "sing."
All of them in old Scotland
But none like margery.

Old Kincaid he called for a blacksmith, too.
All of them could do good work. He used the sledge.
"Ten pounds up," said the blacksmith;
Etc.

Old Kincaid he called for a hunter, too.
All of them could do good work. He blowed a horn.
"Toot, toot, toot," said the hunter;
Etc.

Old Kincaid he called for a woman, too.
All of them could do good work. She used a hoe.
"Hoe, hoe, hoe," said the woman;
Etc.

JENNIE JENKINS

Sung by Rod Drake, Silsbee, Texas, 1952.

"Won't you wear the red?" says Shinaro, Shinaro;
"Won't you wear the red, Jennie Jenkins?"

"Well I won't wear the red,
For that's the color of my head."
To buy me a collar with a double row of circle dircle
Like being row tallow wear did you dare, did you wear
With your robe, Jennie Jenkins?

"Well, won't you wear the blue?" says Shinaro, Shinaro;
"Won't you wear the blue, Jennie Jenkins?"
"I won't wear the blue,
For that's the color of the true."
Etc.

"Oh, won't you wear the purple?" says Shinaro, Shinaro;
"Won't you wear the purple, Jennie Jenkins?"
"Well, I won't wear the purple,
For that's the color of the turtle."
Etc.

"Won't you wear the white?" says Shinaro, Shinaro;
"Won't you wear the white, Jennie Jenkins?"
"Well, I won't wear the white,
For that's the color of the light."
Etc.

"Won't you wear the black?" says Shinaro, Shinaro;
"Won't you wear the black, Jennie Jenkins?"
"Well, I won't wear the black,
For that's the color of my hat."
Etc.

"Won't you wear the light?" says Shinaro, Shinaro;
"Won't you wear the light, Jennie Jenkins?"
"Well, I will wear the light,
For that's the color of the right."
To buy me a tallow with the riff riff riff
To buy me a tallow with a row.

THERE WAS AN OLD MAN THAT LIVED ON THE HILL

This is a version of a Scottish ballad, "John Grumlie." In Texas it is also called "The Grumbler's Song."

Sung by Rod Drake, Silsbee, Texas, 1952.
In stanza four the first two lines are replaced by a spoken text; the last two lines are sung to the music used in the rest of the song for the final lines (C and D).

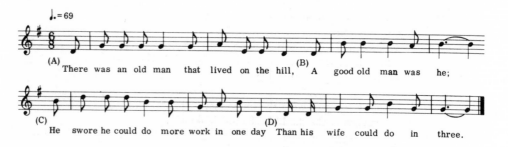

There was an old man that lived on the hill,
A good old man was he;
He swore he could do more work in one day
Than his wife could do in three.

This good old woman, this good old man,
The bargain that we will make:
You go and follow the plow one day
And I'll stay in the house one day.

This good old woman she takened her steps
To go and follow the plow;
This good old man he gathered his pail
To go and milk the cow.

[*Spoken*] Umh. Soo. Steady. Stand still.

The old cow kicked him on top of the head,
And the blood run down to his toes.

He went to feed them three little pigs
That lies in yonder sty,
And the old sow run betwixt his heels
And tossed him ten feet high.

He went to watch the old speckled hen
That she might not lay astray,
And clear forgot the blue mixed yarn
That his wife spun yesterday.

He swore by the moon and by the stars
And by an old green vine
That his wife could do more work in one day
Than he could do in nine.

DEVILISH MARY

Sung by Rod Drake, Silsbee, Texas, 1952.

As I went down to London town
I met up with a handsome lady,
And inquired all around and I got her name
And they called her Devilish Mary.

Refrain:
       Tum a row row day tum a day tum a day
       Tum a row row day tum a day.

Me and Mary got to courtin',
And we got in a hurry,
[*Line 3 missing.*]
And a-married the very next Thursday.
    (*Refrain*)

Mary got so ill and so contrary,
[*Line 2 missing.*]
Ev'ry time I started to work
I had to take it up with Mary.
    (*Refrain*)

Late one day I says to her,
"We'd be the best off parted."
No sooner than I spoke the words
She put on her clothes and started.
    (*Refrain*)

BLUE-EYED BOY IS MAD AT ME

Sung by Rod Drake, Silsbee, Texas, 1952.

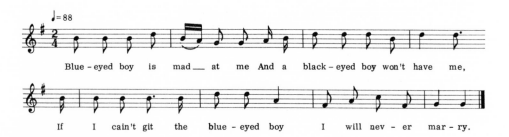

Blue-eyed boy is mad at me
And a black-eyed boy won't have me,
If I cain't git the blue-eyed boy
I will never marry.

Refrain:
    Thank the Lord I'm no man's wife,
    No man cain't control me,

Live and die a single life
Has always been my glory.

Single life is a happy life,
Single life is lovely,
Now I'm single I'm no man's wife,
No man cain't control me.
    (Refrain)

ROLLY TROODUM

Sung by May Kennedy McCord, Springfield, Missouri, 1939. The chords are from the singer's guitar accompaniment.

As I went out a-walking to breathe the pleasant air,
Rolly troodum, troodum, troodum rolly day;
As I went out a-walking to breathe the pleasant air,
I saw a lady talking to her daughter fair,
Rolly troodum, troodum, troodum rolly day.

"Now hush up, dear daughter, and stop your rapid tongue,"
Rolly troodum, troodum, troodum rolly day;
"Now hush up, dear daughter, and stop your rapid tongue,
You're talking about marrying and you know you are too young."
Rolly troodum, troodum, troodum rolly day.

"Now hush up, dear mother, you know I'm a lady grown,"
Rolly troodum, troodum, troodum rolly day;
"Now hush up, dear mother, you know I'm a lady grown,
I've lived seventeen years and I've lived it all alone."
Rolly troodum, troodum, troodum rolly day.

"Oh, if you were to marry who would be your man?"
Rolly troodum, troodum, troodum rolly day;
"Oh, if you were to marry who would be your man?"
"Hush up, mammy, for you know it's handsome Sam."
Rolly troodum, troodum, troodum rolly day.

"They've gone for the parson, the license for to fetch,"
Rolly troodum, troodum, troodum rolly day;
"They've gone for the parson, the license for to fetch,
And I'm going to marry before the sun sets."
Rolly troodum, troodum, troodum rolly day.

"There's doctors and lawyers and men that follow the plough,"
Rolly troodum, troodum, troodum rolly day;
"There's doctors and lawyers and men that follow the plough,
And I'm going to marry, for the fidget's on me now."
Rolly troodum, troodum, troodum rolly day.

"Oh, now my daughter's married and well for to do,"
Rolly troodum, troodum, troodum rolly day;
"Oh, now my daughter's married and well for to do,
So hop along, my jolly boys, I think I'll marry too."
Rolly troodum, troodum, troodum rolly day.

I WISH I WAS A SINGLE GIRL AGAIN

Sung by Maidy Kelly, Livingston, Texas, 1938.

When I was sin - gle Marry-ing was my crave; Now I am mar-ried, Lord, I'm trou-bled to my grave. Gee, I wisht I was a sin - gle girl a - gain.

When I was single
Marrying was my crave;
Now I am married, Lord,
I'm troubled to my grave.
Gee, I wisht I was a single girl again.

Two little children
Lying in the bed,
Both of them so hungry, Lord,
They cain't hold up their heads.
Gee, I wisht I was a single girl again.

Takened in some washing,
Made myself a dollar or two,
My husband slipped around and stoled it,
I don't know what I'll do.
Gee, I wisht I was a single girl again.

Cows are to milk
And the spring's to go to,
No one to help me, Lord,
I have it all to do.
Gee, I wisht I was a single girl again.

I WISH TO MY LORD I WAS SINGLE AGAIN

Sung by R. R. Denoon, Springfield, Missouri, 1939.

I am an old miser all tattered and damned,
From oh, from Ireland and Ireland I came;
I married a maid both twenty and one,
And the very next morning my sorrows begun.

Refrain:

> Oh, what shall I do to get rid of my pain,
> I wish to my Lord I was single again;
> Ever since my coffin was laid
> Before I had married this silly young maid.

Oh, she dresses in satins and silks of all,
She goes to theaters and dances and balls;
Me in my rags and her in her lace,
And some other gentleman comes in my place.
       (Refrain)

THE BLUE-TAILED FLY

One day in June, 1941, I set out with Frank Goodwyn to find a Mexican cowboy who could sing the ballad "El Toro Prieto," the story of a famous black bull on the Norias Ranch. José Gomez at San Perlita was our man; he sang the ballad with some gusto and solemnly affirmed in the last stanza that he had personally witnessed the incidents recounted.

We were recording in Byron Moore's store, and by the time José was through his ballad half the population of San Perlita had gathered to hear and see the miracle of a recording machine. Soon they were urging each other to sing. Byron Moore himself stepped to the microphone and sang "The Blue-Tailed Fly."

I had first heard this song as a play-party game in East Texas, where the people sang it while they danced a regular square dance set. This time there was no dancing, but the audience, from the town marshal to the Mexican cowboys, laughed and clapped, and yelled for more even after I had played the record the third time.

"The Blue-Tailed Fly" was apparently a minstrel song originally. It was published as a penny song sheet in Baltimore in 1846. It may be older than that.

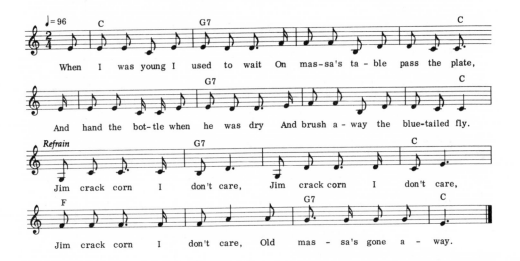

When I was young I used to wait
On massa's table pass the plate,
And hand the bottle when he was dry
And brush away the blue-tailed fly.

Refrain:
    Jim crack corn I don't care,
    Jim crack corn I don't care,
    Jim crack corn I don't care,
    Old massa's gone away.

He rode out one afternoon,
And I followed him with a big whisk-
    broom;
The pony being very shy
Was bitten by a blue-tailed fly.
    (*Refrain*)

They buried him under a 'simmon tree,
And his epitaph was there to see;
Under the ground he's supposed to lie
All by the means of a blue-tailed fly.
    (*Refrain*)

I DON'T LIKE TO SEE BOYS

The tune is "The Irish Washerwoman," as it is for the Negro spiritual "Rock-a My Soul in the Bosom of Abraham."

Sung by Byron Moore, San Perlita, Texas, 1941.

I don't like to see boys away from their mas,
Promenading the streets and puffing cigars;
They ought to be home a-playing with their toys
And saying to each other "I'm one of the boys."

Refrain:
    You may call me kwee,
    You may call me kwy,
    I often say things that's strange to the eye;

But if you don't like it, it's nothing to me,
I'm just saying things that I don't like to see.

I don't like to see girls a-wearing silk dresses,
And the men going around in many distresses;
They ought to be home a-washing the dishes
And patching the holes in their husband's old britches.
(Refrain)

WHO WILL HOLD MY STOVEPIPE HAT

This is a parody of the "Who Will Shoe Your Pretty Little Foot" stanzas in "The Lass of Loch Royal."

Sung by Byron Moore, San Perlita, Texas, 1941.

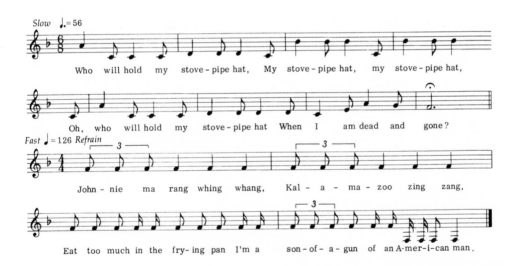

Who will hold my stovepipe hat,
My stovepipe hat, my stovepipe hat,
Oh, who will hold my stovepipe hat
When I am dead and gone?

Refrain:
　Johnnie ma rang whing whang,
　Kalamazoo zing zang,
　Eat too much in the frying pan
　I'm a son-of-a-gun of an American
　　man.

Oh, who will smoke my corncob pipe,
My corncob pipe, my corncob pipe,
Oh, who will smoke my corncob pipe
When I am dead and gone?
　(Refrain)

Oh, who will hold my sweetheart's hand,
My sweetheart's hand, my sweetheart's
　hand,
Oh, who will hold my sweetheart's hand
When I am dead and gone?
　(Refrain)

THE LAZY MAN

Sung by Mrs. Jessie Ann Chennault Smith, Blossom, Texas, 1938.

Come all young people and listen to my song;
I'll tell you of a young man that would-n't hoe his corn,
For the rea-son why I can-not tell, This young man was al-ways well;
For the rea-son why I can-not tell, This young man was al-ways well.

Come all young people and listen to my song;
I'll tell you of a young man that wouldn't hoe his corn,
For the reason why I cannot tell,
This young man was always well;
For the reason why I cannot tell,
This young man was always well.

He went to the cornfield and there he peeped in,
The weeds and grass were up to his chin;
The careless weeds did grow so high,
Made this young man weep and cry;
The careless weeds did grow so high,
Made this young man weep and cry.

He went to his nearest neighbor's house,
Courting as you might suppose;
The conversation did begin,
"Say, young man have you hoed your corn?"
The conversation did begin,
"Say, young man have you hoed your corn?"

He answered her with a sweet reply,
"Yes, my dear, I've laid it by;
For it ain't worth while to strive in vain,
For I don't believe I'll raise one grain;
For it ain't worth while to strive in vain,
For I don't believe I'll raise one grain."

"If you don't believe you'll raise your bread,
Why do you hope to strive to wed?

For single I am and single I'll remain,
A lazy man I won't maintain;
For single I am and single I'll remain,
A lazy man I won't maintain."

Now he's gone to see a widow,
I'm in hopes that he won't git her,
For the rake or a hoe or the handle of a plough
Would suit him much better than a wife just now;
For the rake or a hoe or the handle of a plough
Would suit him much better than a wife just now.

"He cain't raise bread and he cain't get a wife,
Bound to live a bachelor the balance of his life,
For single I am and single I'll remain,
A lazy man I won't maintain;
For single I am and single I'll remain,
A lazy man I won't maintain."

HURRAH FOR ARKANSAS

My mother's family brought this song along with them from Arkansas shortly
after the Civil War. I have not found it elsewhere.

Sung by Mrs. Jessie Ann Chennault Smith, Blossom, Texas, 1938. There is
considerable rhythmic flexibility.

They say there is a stream of crystal waters flow
That'll cure a man sick or well if he will only go.

We're coming, Arkansas, we're coming, Arkansas;
Our four-horse team will soon be seen in the road to Arkansas.

The roads are rough down there, and you will find it so;
There's rocks and rill and rocks and stumps in the road to Arkansas.
We're coming, Arkansas, we're coming, Arkansas;
Our four-horse team will soon be seen in the road to Arkansas.

The men keep hounds down there, and hunting is all they care;
The women they hoe and plough the corn while the men shoot turkey and deer.
Hoorah for Arkansas, hoorah for Arkansas,
You bet your boots we people get there way down in Arkansas.

The girls are strong down there, clean, healthy, and gay;
They card and spin from morning till night and dance from night till day.
Hoorah for Arkansas, hoorah for Arkansas,
Our four-horse team will soon be seen in the road to Arkansas.

They raise their 'baccer patch; the women all smoke and chaw;
Eat hog and hominy and poke for greens way down in Arkansas.
We're leaving Arkansas, we're leaving Arkansas;
Our four-horse teams will never be seen in the hills of Arkansas.

POMPEY SMASH AND DAVY CROCKETT

Pompey Smash and Old Zip Coon were popular characters in minstrel songs before the Civil War. The first part of the song given here is the only version I have found in which Pompey Smash and Old Zip Coon appear together. In a better-known version, "My Polly Ann," sung by Dave Read of Bryant's Minstrels, Pompey Smash marries Polly Ann and retires on her fortune to Baltimore. Davy Crockett, one of the heroes of the Alamo, had become a folk hero before his death and stories about him were in wide circulation. Some unknown singer added the story of Davy Crockett to that of Pompey Smash.

The version included here was sung for me by Lem Jeffus across the street from the Davy Crockett Memorial in Crockett, Texas. To adjust the music to the six-line stanzas, he repeated the first two lines of the four-line stanza for lines three and four, the last two lines remaining the same.

Sung by Lemuel Jeffus, Lovelady, Texas, 1938.

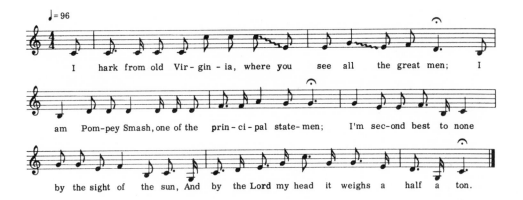

I hark from old Virginia, where you see all the great men;
I am Pompey Smash, one of the principal statemen;
I'm second best to none by the sight of the sun,
And by the Lord my head it weighs a half a ton.

I'll sing to the folks what I think it am concerning,
I'll give you a little touch of the old Virginia learning:
The Yankees say tote and fotch 'stead of bring and carry,
The way to talk grammar by the lord Harry.

There's a nigger that they call Jim Crow, he's a very learned scholar,
Tell you more lies than ever you could swaller;
Says that the world is bigger than the ocean,
Fashagrab's what keeps the world in motion;
Oh, but that is not a fact, for I'll tell you all exact
About the sun and the moon in the twinkling of a crack.

The world is made of mud out of the Mississippi River,
The sun's a ball of foxfire as you all disciver;
The moon's made of cheese, alas it keeps a-flying,
The sun stands still and the world keeps a-gwine;
All the stars are ladies' eyes, all around the world they rise
For to give a little light when the moon don't shine.

Old Zip Coon is what the folks call him;
If ever I catch him I intend for to maul him;
Oh, for such a nigger as he takes a lot of liberty
For to go around the streets and scandalize me.

Said I was a fool and didn't know a letter,
But the folks that know me know a great deal better;
Oh, for such a nigger as he cain't discern true knowledge—
How in the world could he when he's never been to college?
Nor neither have I but I came very nigh,
For I caught a sight of college once as I passed by.

I'll tell you what a time I had with Davy Crockett,
Half horse, half coon, and half sky rocket.
I met Colonel Davy a-going out a-cooning,
Says I, "Davy Crockett, how do you hunt without a gun?"
"Oh," says he, "Pompey Smash, if you'll follow along with Davy,
I'll soon show you how for to grin a coon crazy."

I followed along with Davy till Davy found a squirrel
Sitting on a pine log eating sheep sorrel;
And he stopped right still and for me began to feel;
Says he, "Pompey Smash, let me brace against your heel."

I stuck out my heel for to brace up the sinner,
Old Davy begin to grin a little harder for his dinner.
Oh, at last Davy said, "Oh, he surely must be dead,
For I thought I saw the bark fall around the critter's head."

We both went up for the truth to disciver;
The devil rose to old Pompey Smash's liver;
'Twas a great big knot about the size of a barrel,
Says I, "Davy Crockett, do you call that a squirrel?
And a ha ha ha." "Oh, I'll tell you, black calf, Oh, I tell you you mustn't laugh,
If you do I'll pin your ears back and bite you in half."

I throwed down my gun and I dropped my ammunition.
Says I, "Davy Crockett, I'll cool your ambition."
He backed both ears and he puffed like a steamer;
Says he, "Pompey Smash, I'm a Tennessee screamer."
And we both locked arms and I thought my breath was gone,
For I was never hugged so tight since the day I was born.

We fought half a day and we both agreed to drop it,
For I was badly whipped and so was Davy Crockett.
Come to examine for our heads, gosh, both of them was missing,
For he had bit off my head and I had swallowed his'n;
And we both did agree for to let the other be,
For I was rather hard for him and so was he for me.

JOE BOWERS

No doubt "Joe Bowers" grew out of the California gold rush. It was popular with minstrel singers during the Civil War and had appeared as a penny song sheet at least once by 1860. It lent itself easily to parody. Dichter and Shapiro (*Early American Sheet Music*, p. 123) mention "O I'm a Good Old Rebel. A chaunt to the Hon. Thad. Stevens. Words very Seditious." In a version printed in *Southern Patriotic Songs* Joe Bowers starts to California but gets only as far as Galveston.

There he joins the Confederate Army and is soldiering when his brother's letter reaches him.

Sung by Lemuel Jeffus, Lovelady, Texas, 1939.

My name it is Joe Bowers, ___ I have ___ a bro-ther Ike;
I came ___ from old Mis-sou-ri, ___ Yes, all the way from Pike.
I used to court a pret-ty girl By the name of Sal-ly Black.
I asked her to mar-ry me, She said it was a whack.

My name it is Joe Bowers,
I have a brother Ike;
I came from old Missouri,
Yes, all the way from Pike.
I used to court a pretty girl
By the name of Sally Black.
I asked her to marry me,
She said it was a whack.

But says she to me, "Joe Bowers,
Before we hitch for life,
You'd better get a little house
To keep your little wife."
I said, "Sally, oh, Sally,
It's all for your sake;
I'll go down to California
And try to raise a stake."

At length I went to mining,
Put in my biggest licks;
Fell down upon the shining
Just like a thousand bricks;
I worked both late and early
In rainstorm and snow;
It was all for my dear Sally's sake;
Oh, yes, the same to Joe.

At length there came a letter;
It was from by brother Ike;
It was from old Missouri,
Yes, all the way from Pike.
It had some of the goldarnedest news
A fellow ever heard
That Sally had married a butcher
And the butcher had a red beard.

There was something more in that letter
That would make a fellow swear,
That Sally's got a baby
And the baby's got red hair.

SONGS AND GAMES FOR CHILDREN

FRONTIER CHILDREN had little entertainment except what they provided for themselves or their parents provided for them. Among themselves they said such rhymes as "Eeny meeny miny mo" and "William Trembletoe" as counting out games. At school, when they had school, they played singing games like "London Bridge Is Falling Down," "Marching Round the Levee," and "Farmer in the Dell." At a time when girls were thought to be ready for marriage at fourteen, the last two games could have overtones of courtship. When they sang "Go forth and choose your lover" they might be making the choice of a partner for life.

In many of the homes the childhood years were remarkably brief, and serious. Many families had Bible readings, hymns, and prayers every night and preaching on Sunday. There was little time left for the songs of childhood and, especially among the pious, little inclination to sing them. At best, singing such "old fool songs" was a waste of time. Fortunate were the children whose families had a tradition of singing songs not heard in church.

Some of the songs in this section made the long journey from early Britain to the Texas frontier, from hunting the wren and Reynard the Fox to the nonsense of "Way down South where I was born" and of the lines from "Old Jay Bird":

> Old jay bird sittin' on a limb,
> He winked at me and I winked at him.
> Picked up a rock and I hit him on the shin;
> Says he, "Young man, don't you do that agin."

134

COME ALL YOU JOLLY HUNTERS

Sung by Rod Drake, Silsbee, Texas, 1952.

Come all you jolly hunters
Who'd like to chase a fox
And we'll chase old poor Rambler
All amongst them hills and rocks.

Refrain:
    And a woop woop woop woop foddler
    All in the morning soon
    Tum a ran ran ran
    Tum a dippy dippy dan
    And away we'll rove all over
    And a bugle lee
    And a high tippy tippy and a uty oh
    And through the woods we'll run our boys
    And through the woods we'll run them.

Well, the first was a maiden
A-combing her golden locks

And I thought I heard her say, "Oh, poor Rambler,
All amongst them hills and rocks."
    (Refrain)

Well, the next was a teamster
A-yoking up his team
And I thought I heard him say, "Oh, poor Rambler,
A-floating down stream."
    (Refrain)

FROG WENT A-COURTING

Almost any schoolchild in Texas can sing a version of this old song. It is one of our oldest folk songs, having been traced in documents back to the time of Henry VIII. The version printed here seems to be a composite of "Frog Went A-Courting" and "Frog in the Well." The nonsense refrain possibly came originally from a minstrel song called "Kitty Kimbo."

a. Sung by Rod Drake, Silsbee, Texas, 1952.

The strong emphasis of B♮ and C♯ is most unusual in a tune whose opening and closing phrases establish F as the most important note.

Frog went a-courting, he did ride, mhmh,
Frog went a-courting, he did ride,
A sword and a pistol a-hanging to his side, mhmh.

Rode up to Miss Mouse's gate, mhmh,
Rode up to Miss Mouse's gate,
"Pray, kind Miss, will you marry with me, mhmh?"

"No, kind Sir, I cain't answer that, mhmh,
No, kind Sir, I cain't answer that
Without relief from old Uncle Rat, mhmh."

Old Uncle Rat he's gone to town, mhmh,
Old Uncle Rat he's gone to town
To buy his niece a wedding gown, mhmh.

Old Uncle Flea he's gone there, too, mhmh,
Old Uncle Flea he's gone there, too,
To buy his niece a pair of shoes, mhmh.

Old Mister Rat come a-hustling home, mhmh,
Old Mister Rat come a-hustling home.
"Who's been here since I've been gone, mhmh?"

"Very fine gentleman," she did say, mhmh,
"Very fine gentleman," she did say,
"And he asked me for to marry him, mhmh."

Old Uncle Rat laughed and he shook his fat side, mhmh,
Old Uncle Rat laughed and he shook his fat side
To think his niece was gonna be a bride, mhmh.

"Where's your wedding supper gonna be, mhmh?
Where's your wedding supper gonna be?"
"Away down yonder in a hollow tree, mhmh."

"What you gonna have for your wedding supper, mhmh?
What you gonna have for your wedding supper?"
"Two blue beans and a black-eyed pea, mhmh."

Well, the first come in was Missis Flea, mhmh,
The first come in was Missis Flea,
She swore she'd do a jig with a bumblebee, mhmh.

Next come in was a bumblebee, mhmh,
Next come in was a bumblebee,
Played his fiddle on his knee, mhmh.

The next come in was a July bug, mhmh,
Next come in was a July bug,
A little bitty dram and a great big jug, mhmh.

Next come in was a July fly, mhmh,
Next come in was a July fly,
If he didn't have a gallon I wisht I may die, mhmh.

Next come in was an old sly cat, mhmh,
Next come in was an old sly cat,
She swore, by Joe, she'd put 'em out of that, mhmh.

Old Mister Rat went scaling up the wall, mhmh,
Old Mister Rat went scaling up the wall.
Don't you think that bride'll fall, mhmh?

Old Mister Frog went swimming across the brook, mhmh,
Old Mister Frog went swimming across the brook,
A big black snake took him down his crook, mhmh.

b. Sung by May Kennedy McCord, Springfield, Missouri, 1939.

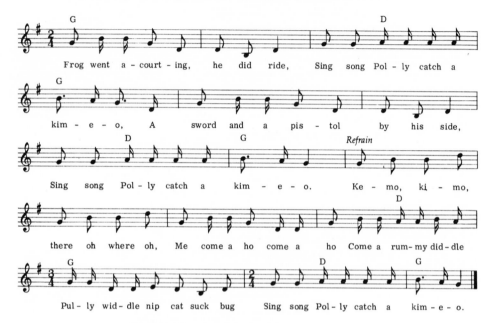

Frog went a-courting, he did ride,
Sing song Polly catch a kimeo,
A sword and a pistol by his side,
Sing song Polly catch a kimeo.

Refrain:
        Kemo, kimo, there oh where oh,
        Me come a ho come a ho
        Come a rummy diddle
        Pully widdle nip cat suck bug
        Sing song Polly catch a kimeo.

He rode till he came to the mouse's door,
Sing song Polly catch a kimeo,
Said he, "Miss Mouse, are you within?"
Sing song Polly catch a kimeo.
        (*Refrain*)

He took the mouse upon his knee,
Sing song Polly catch a kimeo,
Says he, "My dear, will you marry me?"
Sing song Polly catch a kimeo.
        (*Refrain*)

"I first must ask Mr. Rat's consent,"
Sing song Polly catch a kimeo,

"Or else I could not live content."
Sing song Polly catch a kimeo.
(Refrain)

Old Mr. Rat laughed and shook his fat sides
Sing song Polly catch a kimeo,
To think Miss Mousie would be a bride.
Sing song Polly catch a kimeo.
(Refrain)

Oh, where will the wedding supper be?
Sing song Polly catch a kimeo,
Down in the meadow by the whiteoak tree.
Sing song Polly catch a kimeo.
(Refrain)

Oh, what will the wedding supper be?
Sing song Polly catch a kimeo,
Two black beans and a bumblebee.
Sing song Polly catch a kimeo.
(Refrain)

Old Mr. Rat began to sing;
Sing song Polly catch a kimeo,
The old cat and kittens came a-tumbling in.
Sing song Polly catch a kimeo.
(Refrain)

WAY DOWN SOUTH WHERE I WAS BORN

Sung by Rod Drake, Silsbee, Texas, 1952.

Way down south where I was born, Sing song Kit-ty cain't you kim-ey-o,—

Kee-mo, ki-mo sing o where, Sing song Kit-ty cain't you kim-ey-o.

Refrain

Kee-mo ki-mo sing o where m-hee m-hy m-ho m-nipcat

pen-ny wink-y nip cat song Sing song Kit-ty cain't you kim-ey-o.

Way down south where I was born,
Sing song Kitty cain't you kimeyo,
Keemo, kimo sing o where,
Sing song Kitty cain't you kimeyo.

Refrain:

Keemo kimo sing o where
m-hee m-hy m-ho m-nipcat penny winky nip cat song
Sing song Kitty cain't you kimeyo.

Oh, skeeters and gnats is a-gittin' mighty bold,
Sing song Kitty cain't you kimeyo,
Keemo, kimo sing o where
Sing song Kitty cain't you kimeyo.
(*Refrain*)

Fish in the dairy nine days old,
Sing song Kitty cain't you kimeyo,
Keemo, kimo sing o where
Song song Kitty cain't you kimeyo.
(*Refrain*)

There was a fish and his name was whale,
Sing song Kitty cain't you kimeyo,
Swallowed Jonah head and tail
Sing song Kitty cain't you kimeyo.
(*Refrain*)

Shanghai chicken he growed so tall,
Sing song Kitty cain't you kimeyo,
Growed so tall that you couldn't hear him crow,
Song song Kitty cain't you kimeyo.
(*Refrain*)

WHEN I'SE A LITTLE BOY

Sung by Rod Drake, Silsbee, Texas, 1952.

When I'se a lit-tle boy fat as I could grow, [Whistle] When

I'se a lit-tle boy fat as I could grow, Set-ting on a toy bench

side for a show Sing-ing ty wink-y-ty wink-y a.____

When I'se a little boy fat as I could grow,
[*Whistle*]
When I'se a little boy fat as I could grow,
Setting on a toy bench side for a show
Singing ty winkyty winky a.

Long came a John,
[*Whistle*]
Long came a John,
Beat on his [*inaudible*]
Kill him with his gun
Singing ty winkyty winky a.

Everybody saw what a deed I'd done,
[*Whistle*]
Everybody saw what a deed I'd done,
He give me a little money, about three thousand tons,
Singing ty winkyty winky a.

I made a little box about three acres square,
[*Whistle*]
I made a little box about three acres square,
And in my box I put my money there,
Singing ty winkyty winky a.

Whenever I traveled I traveled like an ox,
[*Whistle*]
Whenever I traveled I traveled like an ox,
In my vest pocket I carried my little box,
Singing ty winkyty winky a.

Had an old hen and her color was fair,
[*Whistle*]
Had an old hen and her color was fair,
Set her on a mussel shell, hatched out a hare,
Singing ty winkyty winky a.

Hatched into a horse about six feet high,
[*Whistle*]
Hatched into a horse about six feet high,
And if anybody beats that I'll know they told a lie,
Singing ty winkyty winky a.

PRETTIEST LITTLE TREE

Sung by Rod Drake, Silsbee, Texas, 1952.

Prettiest little tree that you ever seen
The tree in the woods and the woods on the ground,
Round, round, round, round,
Green grass growed all around.

On the little leaf there was a little nest,
Prettiest little nest that you ever seen
A nest on a leaf and a leaf on a twig
And a twig on a limb and a limb on a tree
And the tree in the woods and the woods in the ground,
Round, round, round, round,
Green grass growed all around.

In the little nest there was a little egg,
Prettiest little egg that you ever seen,
Egg in the nest and the nest on a leaf,
Etc.

In the little egg there was a little elephant,
Prettiest little elephant that you ever seen,
Elephant in the egg and the egg in the nest,
Etc.

On the little elephant there was a little snout,
Prettiest little snout that you ever seen,
A snout on the elephant and the elephant in the egg,
Etc.

On the little snout there was a little skeeter,
Prettiest little skeeter that you ever seen,
Skeeter on the snout and the snout on the elephant,
Etc.

On the little skeeter there was a little cap,
Prettiest little cap that you ever seen,
Cap on the skeeter and the skeeter on the snout,
Etc.

HUNTING THE WREN

"Hunting the Wren" was the first song I knew. My mother sang it to me as a nursery song, and my brothers sang it as a game.

The history of this song is unusual. Its connection with the celebration of St. Stephen's Day has been reported in various collections of English and Irish folklore. Though that connection has been entirely lost in Texas, the following passage (*Journal*, VI, 263) will interest persons who have thought of "Hunting the Wren" only as a nursery song:

St. Stephen's Day—It is considered lucky to have been born on St. Stephen's Day, the 26th of December, though why I do not know. Any one abstaining from eating meat on this day, in honor of our first martyr, will not catch any contagious disease during the year. We never ate any meat on this day, and consequently never were afflicted with contagious diseases.

On Christmas Day boys from ten to twenty years of age catch the wren in the furze hedge,—for it is said to be blind on this day,—and early next morning they carry these little prisoners in a box or basket from door to door, asking for money to bury the wren. One of the boys, dressed like a clown and playing a fife or horn, heads the procession, the others calling out or singing:

The wren, the wren, the king of all birds,
On St. Stephen's Day he was caught in the furze.
Up with the kettle, and down with the pan,
Give us an answer and let us began.

Any one refusing to give money, for which the boys always ask, was punished by having the wren buried by his door. This would bring bad luck to the inmates of his home. On the night of the same day the boys, using the money collected, would have a jollification, the older ones usually going to town and getting on a spree.

Sung by William A. Owens.

"Let's go hunt-ing," said Rob-sha-Bob; "Let's go hunt-ing," said Ridge to Rodge;

"Let's go hunt-ing," said Dan-iel Joe; "Let's go hunt-ing," said Bil-ly Bar-low.

"Let's go hunting," said Rob-sha-Bob;
"Let's go hunting," said Ridge to Rodge;
"Let's go hunting," said Daniel Joe;
"Let's go hunting," said Billy Barlow.

"What shall we hunt?" said Rob-sha-Bob;
"What shall we hunt?" said Ridge to
          Rodge;
"What shall we hunt?" said Daniel Joe;
"What shall we hunt?" said Billy Barlow.

"Go hunt a wren," said Rob-sha-Bob;
"Go hunt a wren," said Ridge to Rodge;
"Go hunt a wren," said Daniel Joe;
"Go hunt a wren," said Billy Barlow.

"How'll we kill it?" said Rob-sha-Bob;
"How'll we kill it?" said Ridge to Rodge;
"How'll we kill it?" said Daniel Joe;
"How'll we kill it?" said Billy Barlow.

"Go borrow a gun," said Rob-sha-Bob;
"Go borrow a gun," said Ridge to Rodge;

"Go borrow a gun," said Daniel Joe;
"Go borrow a gun," said Billy Barlow.

"How'll we cook it?" said Rob-sha-Bob;
"How'll we cook it?" said Ridge to Rodge;
"How'll we cook it?" said Daniel Joe;
"How'll we cook it?" said Billy Barlow.

"Go borrow a skillet," said Rob-sha-Bob;
"Go borrow a skillet," said Ridge to Rodge;
"Go borrow a skillet," said Daniel Joe;
"Go borrow a skillet," said Billy Barlow.

"How'll we divide it?" said Rob-sha-Bob;
"How'll we divide it?" said Ridge to
          Rodge;
"How'll we divide it?" said Daniel Joe;
"How'll we divide it?" said Billy Barlow.

"I'll take the head," said Rob-sha-Bob;
"I'll take the back," said Ridge to Rodge;
"I'll take the breast," said Daniel Joe;
"I'll take the rest," said Billy Barlow.

SAW AN OLD CROW

Sung by Mrs. Imogene Hyde, Calvert, Texas, 1938.

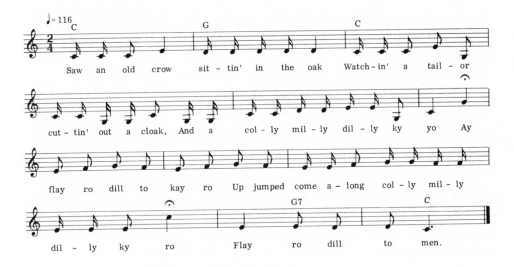

Saw an old crow sittin' in the oak
Watchin' a tailor cuttin' out a cloak,
And a colly milly dilly ky yo
Ay flay ro dill to kay ro
Up jumped come along colly milly dilly ky ro
Flay ro dill to men.

Me and my wife sprang to the house
To make some cool blood pudding and a souse,
And a colly milly dilly ky yo
Ay flay ro dill to kay ro
Up jumped come along colly milly dilly ky yo
Flay ro dill to men.

OLD JAY BIRD

Mrs. Imogene Hyde of Calvert, who recorded this song for me, said her family had learned it from Negro workers on Brazos bottoms plantations many years ago. The first part is from a popular humorous song, while the refrain apparently came from a nineteenth-century minstrel song. "Old Jay Bird" is also known in Texas as a play-party song.

Sung by Mrs. Imogene Hyde, Calvert, Texas, 1938.

Old jay bird sittin' on a limb,
He winked at me and I winked at him.
Picked up a rock and I hit him on the shin;
Says he, "Young man, don't you do that agin."

Kay, Jim-along, Jim-along, Josie,
Kay, Jim-along, Jim-along Joe.
Kay, Jim-along, Jim-along, Josie,
Kay, Jim-along, Jim-along Joe.

THE BROWN DUCK

This song is of English origin, and as "Bold Reynard Fox" was published in broadside form in the eighteenth century. It is known throughout America.

Sung by William A. Owens.

The fox jumped up one moonlight night;
Called to the moon to give him light;
He had a long way to go that night
Before he could reach his den, O,
Den, O, den, O, he had a long way to go that night
Before he could reach his den O.

He took the brown duck by the neck,
Slung her over across his back,
The brown duck cried, "Quack, quack, quack,
The fox is off to his den, O."
Den, O, den, O, he had a long way to go that night
Before he could reach his den O.

Old Mother Flip-Flop jumped out of bed,
Raised up the window and popped out her head,
"Run, John, run, the brown duck's gone,
The fox is off to his den, O."
Den, O, den, O, he had a long way to go that night
Before he could reach his den O.

John went running across the hill,
Blowing his horn both loud and shrill,
But the fox kept on running still
Till he had reached his den, O.
Den, O, den, O, he had a long way to go that night
Before he could reach his den O.

He took the brown duck home to his wife,
They ate her without a fork or knife,
They never tasted anything better in their life,
And the little ones ate the bones, O.
Bones, O, bones, O, they never tasted anything better in their life,
And the little ones ate the bones O.

PLAY-PARTY
SONGS AND GAMES

THE FIDDLE SURVIVED the migration from the British Isles to the American frontier and for some was almost as important as the Bible, the gun, and the plow. Bagpipes did not. A whittler could whittle out a fiddle of wood and string it with dried cat-gut, and many did, some so ineptly that echoes of caterwauling lingered on. Still, the fiddler was able to play an Irish jig or a Scottish hornpipe well enough for people to dance to.

Dance they did, though in many a frontier community where religious fervor ran high dancing was listed among the deadly sins. Preachers regarded the fiddle as the instrument of the devil and preached against it. In spite of them dancing flourished and frontiersmen, improvising in music and step, created the square dance.

Folk dancing had already been discovered and moved, refined and styled, from the country to city ballrooms. These dances came in this form to the American cities while the country originals found their way to the frontier. Dancers on the frontier forgot the routines. A caller who could call the steps became as essential as the fiddler, and together they evolved what became the American square dance. Only loosely related to European routines, the American calls were free and easy and subject to the caller's imagination. Such European forms as *promenade* and *sashay* gradually changed from a mincing step to a rough boot stomp.

The caller's words soon reflected American experience, American humor. The invitation to the dance often appeared in crude words:

> Get your partner, hit her on the head;
> If she don't like biscuit, feed her cornbread.

The elaborate bow became not at all elaborate:

148

> Bow to your partner, bow to your taw,
> Bow to that gal from Arkansas.

In frontier communities where square dancing was absolutely forbidden, people who wanted to dance turned their backs on fiddler and caller and danced to their own singing. Songs with lively rhythms abounded. Dance calls could easily be set to them. Thus in their ingenuity people on the frontier created the play-party. Play-party songs became a combination of the caller's art and the frontier experience. Singers had much freedom of expression. They could use actual names of people present as well as names of places and regions. Play-parties did not entirely escape the mark of sin. In "The Wicked Daughter" the line occurs: "She went to parties both dance and play." Preachers preached against them but rarely demanded that a young person guilty of going to a play-party be "churched."

Preached against or not, play-party games are a form of dancing. The calls sung are variations of square dance calls, or of the "longways dance," the Virginia reel. The rhythm is a dance rhythm very close to that of the "breakdown" fiddle tune. A square dance call like "Wave the ocean, wave the sea, wave that pretty girl back to me" is traditional; so is the play-party call "First to the right and then to the left, and then to the girl that he loves best."

In this volume the descriptions of games that accompany the songs have been omitted. Some of the tunes from my earlier book *Swing and Turn: Texas Play-Party Games* have been transposed and the meter altered so that the quarter-note or dotted quarter-note always gets the beat.

SHOOT THE BUFFALO

a. [*Singer unidentified*]

Rise you up, my dearest dear,
And present to me your hand,
And we'll all run away
To some fair and distant land.

Refrain:

Where the ladies knit and sew,
And the gents they plow and hoe,
We'll ramble in the canebreak
And shoot the buffalo.

Oh, the rabbit shot the monkey,
And the monkey shot the crow;
Let us ramble through the canebreak
And shoot the buffalo.
        (Refrain)

All the way from Georgia
To Texas I must go,
To rally 'round the canebreak
And shoot the buffalo.
        (Refrain)

b. Sung by Rod Drake, Silsbee, Texas, 1952.

Oh, rise you up my love,
And present to me your hand,
And we'll take a ramble over
In some far and distant land.

And the hawk shot the buzzard,
And the buzzard shot the crow,
And we rambled all together,
And we chased the buffalo.

I'M ON MY WAY TO GEORGY

Sung by Rod Drake, Silsbee, Texas, 1952.

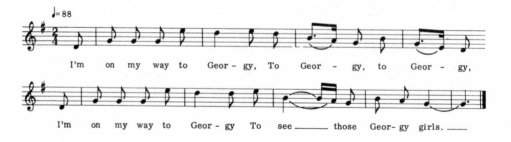

I'm on my way to Georgy,
To Georgy, to Georgy,
I'm on my way to Georgy
To see those Georgy girls.

My father upholds me,
Upholds me, upholds me;
My father upholds me
And gives me a horse to ride.

Oh, my mother she scold me,
She scold me, she scold me;
My mother she scold me
For fooling with the Georgy gals.

Oh, swing another'n in, and swing another'n in,
And swing another'n in, and swing another'n in,
Swing another'n in, and swing another'n in
Before it's too late.

I'm on my way to Georgy,
To Georgy, to Georgy;
I'm on my way to Georgy
To see those Georgy girls.

Oh, swing another'n in, and swing another'n in,
And swing another'n in, and swing another'n in,
Swing another'n in, and swing another'n in
Before it's too late.

WEEVILY WHEAT

I don't want none of your weevily wheat,
And I don't want none of your barley;
I want some flour and half an hour
To bake a cake for Charlie.

Weevily wheat's not fit to eat,
Neither is her barley;
A sack of flour and half an hour
To bake a cake for Charlie.

Charlie's here and Charlie's there,
And Charlie's over the ocean;
Charlie won't come home again
Until he takes a notion.

Charlie he's a fine young man,
Charlie he's a dandy;
Charlie he's the same young man
Who fed the girls on candy.

Who's been here since I've been gone
Around the fields of barley;
A pretty little girl with red shoes on
To bake a cake for Charlie.

Charlie he's a nice young man,
Charlie he's a dandy;
Charlie he's the very young man
That stole old Buck and Brandy.

Five times five is twenty-five,
Six times five is thirty,
Seven times five is thirty-five,
And eight times five is forty;

Nine times five is forty-five,
Ten times five is fifty,
Eleven times five is fifty-five,
And twelve times five is sixty.

Trading boats have gone ashore,
Trading boats are landing,
Trading boats have gone ashore,
Loaded down with candy.

Way down yonder in the maple swamp,
Where the water's deep and muddy,
We'll dance and sing till broad daylight,
And won't get home till Sunday.

If you love me like I love you
We'll have no time to tarry;
We'll have the old folks flying around
Fixing for us to marry.

Charlie Cole is a good old soul,
Charlie he's a dandy;
Charlie Cole is the very old soul
That drank up all my brandy.

LITTLE BRASS WAGON

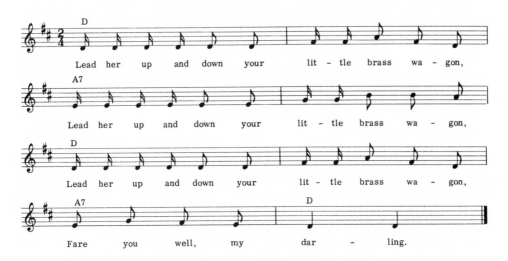

Lead her up and down your little brass wagon,
Lead her up and down your little brass wagon,
Lead her up and down your little brass wagon,
Fare you well, my darling.

One wheel off and the axle dragging, *etc.*

Two wheels off the little brass wagon, *etc.*

Three wheels off the little brass wagon, *etc.*

Four wheels off the little brass wagon, *etc.*

Swing and turn the little brass wagon, *etc.*

Around and around the little brass wagon, *etc.*

All promenade in the little brass wagon, *etc.*

THE GIRL I LEFT BEHIND ME

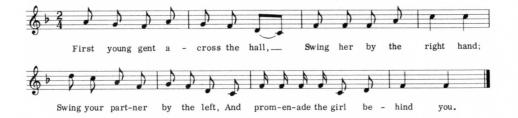

First young gent across the hall,   Oh, the girl, the pretty little girl,
Swing her by the right hand;   The girl I left behind me,
Swing your partner by the left,   Rosy cheeks and curly hair,
And promenade the girl behind you.   The girl I left behind me.

GOING TO BOSTON

Ha-ha ——, I'll tell your mama,
Ha-ha ——, I'll tell your mama,
Ha-ha ——, I'll tell your mama,
That you're going to marry.

Come on, girls, let's go to Boston, [three times]
To see this couple marry.

Come on, boys, you can go with us, [three times]
To see this couple marry.

Ha-ha ——, I'll tell your papa, [three times]
That you're going to marry.

Come on, boys, let's go to Boston, [three times]
To see this couple marry.

Come on, girls, you can go with us, [three times]
To see this couple marry.

Now they're married and living in Boston, [three times]
Living on chicken pie.

OLD DAN TUCKER

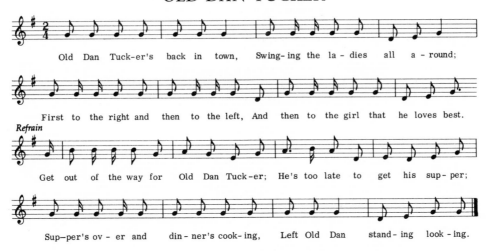

Old Dan Tuck-er's back in town, Swing-ing the la-dies all a-round;

First to the right and then to the left, And then to the girl that he loves best.

Refrain

Get out of the way for Old Dan Tuck-er; He's too late to get his sup-per;

Sup—per's ov-er and din-ner's cook-ing, Left Old Dan stand-ing look-ing.

Old Dan Tucker's back in town,
Swinging the ladies all around;
First to the right and then to the left,
And then to the girl that he loves best.

Refrain:
 Get out of the way for Old Dan
  Tucker;
 He's too late to get his supper;
 Supper's over and dinner's cooking,
 Left Old Dan standing looking.

Old Dan Tucker, big and fat,
Washed his face in my straw hat,
Dried his face on a wagon wheel,
Died with the toothache in the heel.
 (Refrain)

Old Dan Tucker's mother-in-law
Was the ugliest thing I ever saw:
Her eyes stuck out and her nose stuck in,
Her upper lip hung over her chin.
 (Refrain)

Old Dan Tucker was a fine old man,
He washed his face in a frying pan;
He combed his hair with a wagon wheel
And died with the toothache in his heel.

Refrain:
 Clear the track for Old Dan Tucker,
 He's too late to get his supper;
 Supper's over and dinner's cooking,
 Left Old Dan standing looking.

HOG-DROVERS

Hog-drov-ers, hog-drov-ers, hog-drov-ers we are, A-court-ing your

daugh-ter so rare and so fair. Can we get lodg-ing

here-o-here? Can we get lodg-ing here?

Hog-drovers, hog-drovers, hog-drovers we are,
A-courting your daughter so rare and so fair.
Can we get lodging here-o-here?
Can we get lodging here?

This is my daughter who sits by my side,
And none of you hog-drovers can get her for his bride,
And you can't get lodging here-o-here,
And you can't get lodging here.

Mighty pretty daughter but ugly yourself,
So we'll march onward and better ourselves,
And we don't want lodging here-o-here,
And we don't want lodging here.

This is my daughter who sits by my side,
And Mr. —— can make her his bride
If he'll bring me another one here-o-here,
If he'll bring me another one here.

DANCE JOSEY

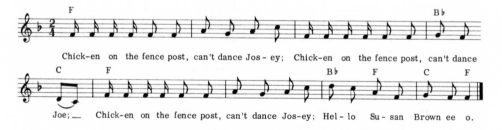

Chicken on the fence post, can't dance Josey;
Chicken on the fence post, can't dance Joe;
Chicken on the fence post, can't dance Josey;
Hello Susan Brown ee o.

Choose your partner and come dance Josey; *etc.*

Chew my gum while I dance Josey; *etc.*

Shoestring's broke and I can't dance Josey; *etc.*

Hold my mule while I dance Josey; *etc.*

Crank my Ford while I dance Josey; *etc.*

Hair in the butter, can't dance Josey; *etc.*

Brier in my heel, can't dance Josey; *etc.*

Stumped my toe, can't jump Josey; *etc.*

OLD JOE CLARK

a. [*Singer unidentified*]

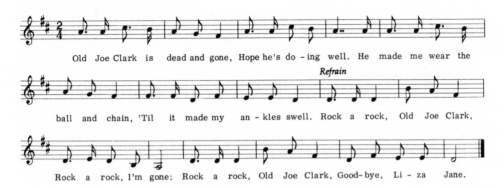

Old Joe Clark is dead and gone, Hope he's doing well. He made me wear the
ball and chain, 'Til it made my ankles swell. Rock a rock, Old Joe Clark,
Rock a rock, I'm gone; Rock a rock, Old Joe Clark, Good-bye, Liza Jane.

Old Joe Clark is dead and gone,
Hope he's doing well.
He made me wear the ball and chain,
'Til it made my ankles swell.

Refrain:
  Rock a rock, Old Joe Clark,
  Rock a rock, I'm gone;
  Rock a rock, Old Joe Clark,
  Good-bye Liza Jane.

Wish I had a great big house
Sixteen stories high,
And every story in that house
Was filled with chicken pie.
  (*Refrain*)

Used to be a little boy
Playing in the ashes;
Now I am a great big boy
Wearing Dad's mustaches.
  (*Refrain*)

Used to be a little girl
Playing in the sand;
Now I am a great big girl

All I need's a man.
  (*Refrain*)

I went down to Old Joe Clark's,
Never been there before;
He slept on a feather bed,
And I slept on the floor.
  (*Refrain*)

Massa had an old gray horse;
Rode him down to town,
Before he could get his trading done
The buzzards had him down.
  (*Refrain*)

I went down to Old Joe Clark's
Him and his wife wasn't home;
Got in a fight with the oldest girl
And broke her tucking comb.
  (*Refrain*)

Old Joe Clark has two girls,
Both are dressed in red;
Every time I see those girls
I wish my wife was dead.
  (*Refrain*)

Old Joe Clark had a yellow cat,
She would neither sing nor pray;
She stuck her head in a buttermilk jar
And washed her sins away.
    (Refrain)

Massa had a yaller gal;
He fotched her from the South;
She wropped her hair so very tight
She could not shut her mouth.
    (Refrain)

I wish I was in Arkansas,
A-sitting on a rail,
A jug of whiskey under my arm
And a 'possum by the tail.
    (Refrain)

If you see that girl of mine,
Tell her if you please,
When she starts to make up bread
To roll them dirty sleeves.
    (Refrain)

I went down to Old Joe Clark's,
Thought I'd go a-hunting;

I fell down and broke my back,
Came back home a-grunting.
    (Refrain)

Old Joe Clark has got a mule,
His name is Morgan Brown,
And every tooth that mule has got
Is sixteen inches 'round.
    (Refrain)

Joe Clark's mule is dead and gone,
I'll tell you where I found him;
Away down in the barley patch,
With the buzzards all around him.
    (Refrain)

You can ride the old gray mare,
I will ride the roan;
You can talk to your sweetheart,
I'll talk to my own.
    (Refrain)

I went over to Old Joe Clark's;
He invited me in to supper;
I stumped my toe on the table leg
And stuck my nose in the butter.
    (Refrain)

b. Sung by Maidy Kelly, Livingston, Texas, 1941.

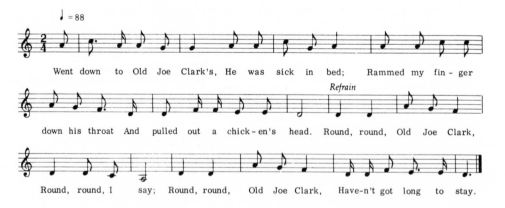

Went down to Old Joe Clark's, He was sick in bed; Rammed my fin-ger down his throat And pulled out a chick-en's head. Round, round, Old Joe Clark, Round, round, I say; Round, round, Old Joe Clark, Have-n't got long to stay.

Went down to Old Joe Clark's,
He was sick in bed;
Rammed my finger down his throat
And pulled out a chicken's head.

Refrain:
    Round, round, Old Joe Clark,
    Round, round, I say;
    Round, round, Old Joe Clark,
    Haven't got long to stay.

Went down to my new ground,
Guess what I saw:
Sixteen blackbirds a-pulling my plow
And the jaybird hollering, "Haw."
    (*Refrain*)

Sixteen chickens on the fence
All a-trying to crow;

Dead man trying to shave hisself,
Blind man trying to sew.
    (*Refrain*)

Went down to Old Joe Clark's,
He was doing well,
Made me wear ball and chain
Made my ankles swell.
    (*Refrain*)

BUFFALO GIRLS

Buffalo girls, won't you come out tonight,
Won't you come out tonight, won't you come out tonight;
Buffalo girls, won't you come out tonight,
And dance by the light of the moon.

Oh, I danced with a girl with a hole in her stocking,
And her toe kept a-rocking, and her heel kept a-knocking;
Oh, I danced with a girl with a hole in her stocking,
The prettiest girl in the room.

SKIP TO MY LOU

Flies in the buttermilk, skip to my Lou;
Flies in the buttermilk, skip to my Lou;
Flies in the buttermilk, skip to my Lou,
Skip to my Lou, my darling.

Gone again, skip to my Lou; *etc.*

Stole my partner, what'll I do? *etc.*

I'll get another one prettier than you; *etc.*

Little red wagon painted blue; *etc.*

Left again, skip to my Lou; *etc.*

Stand there, Big Foot, and don't know what to do; *etc.*

Chicken on the haystack, shoo, shoo, shoo; *etc.*

Rat's in the buttermilk, skip to my Lou; *etc.*

TIDEO

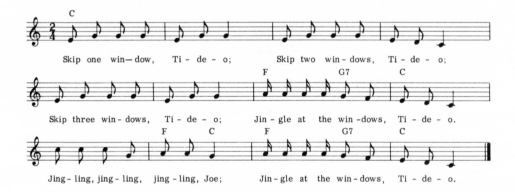

Skip one window, Tideo;
Skip two windows, Tideo;
Skip three windows, Tideo;
Jingle at the windows, Tideo.
Jingling, jingling, jingling, Joe;
Jingle at the windows, Tideo.

ANGLO-AMERICAN SPIRITUALS

IN TEXAS, as in other parts of the South, two streams of religious folk music—the white spiritual and the Negro spiritual—persist side by side, especially in rural pockets, where they are separate but closely related, the second a tide out of the first. Folklorists have tended to record and study the Negro spiritual and ignore the white, to the neglect of a rich vein of American folk music, at times to the neglect of the true kinship between Anglo-American and Afro-American music.

Many of the white spirituals had their origins in the songs of open dissent in Britain, many in the works of such hymn-makers as Isaac Watts, John Newton, and William Cowper. They were brought to America in books and also in the memories of settlers. In Massachusetts these hymns eventually supplanted *The Bay Psalm Book.* In Virginia, in the Anglican church, they found a place alongside but did not replace the English plainsong. On the frontier they were widely accepted, and as secular music underwent change, so did religious music.

In the Appalachians and farther west, beyond the reach of the established churches, beyond the reach of printed liturgies, preachers preached and people sang of the fears of hell, the hope of heaven, and an intensely personal relationship with God. Preachers, often unlettered, made up sermons on the spot. Singers, fully as unlettered, also improvised. They sang songs as they remembered them, and memory often served them poorly; or they changed them to embody new religious experience, or sought new communion with their God and with their brethren. Under the same circumstances new songs came into being, some to survive. West of the Blue Ridge Mountains these songs preceded harmonic instruments by almost a hundred years, and song books by almost as many. As a result these frontier creations lacked conformity in both poetic and musical form, but not in religious fervor, which ran deeply to the evangelical.

When songs for a meeting had worn thin the preacher often turned to "lining" out. The device was simple. With book or Bible in hand he would name a song or scripture and "h'ist" the pitch of some old tune. Then he would read a line and join the congregation in singing it. The spoken word, the sung response, led rather easily into a kind of communal composition in which a leader spoke or sang a question and the congregation sang a response. Thus new words were created for an old hymn tune, an old ballad tune, or a new tune rising spontaneously. The several tunes of "Barbara Allen" lent themselves easily to religious words. So did the well-known tune of "The Three Black Crows," which became the tune of a religious song and of the war song "When Johnny Comes Marching Home." To make a new song unto the Lord the singer often resorted to intermingling of religious and secular to the extent that only phrases of either remained.

By the time the wave of revivalism began in Kentucky in the early part of the nineteenth century, there was a large body of spirituals that traveled from camp meeting to camp meeting, brush arbor to brush arbor, first orally and then in hymn —called "church song"—books. These spirituals are generally associated with the rural South, but many of them traveled to the North. The music, when it was printed at all, was usually printed in shape notes rather than the round of lines and spaces, because singers could memorize the shapes and read with what they considered greater facility.

Dozens of "harmonies" were printed in shape notes in the nineteenth century, as George Pullen Jackson has shown in his *White Spirituals in the Southern Uplands*. In the early twentieth century most of the hymnals printed for use in rural churches and many of those for urban churches retained the shape notes. Some of the more popular hymnals are still available in both round and shape notes.

Songs not strictly hymns were sung sometimes in churches and often in "singings" in homes. Usually in ballad form, these songs were both moral and emotional. Among those sung in Texas into the twentieth century were "The Wicked Daughter," "The Orphan Girl," and "The Romish Lady."

With increasing urbanization and commercial publication of songbooks for church worship, many white spirituals faded from use and sank into oblivion. Those that found their way into the "harmonies" were preserved in print but not in use. Few found their way into the more sophisticated hymnbooks. Even fewer were rescued by composers and given a place in traditional church music.

The white spirituals included here, a handful out of the hundreds that were once a part of the oral tradition, are remembered from brush arbor revivals and "singings" in the East Texas of half a century ago. Led by the preacher, sung without accompaniment, they were mournful reminders of man's earthly conditions and heavenly hope.

THE HEBREW CHILDREN

Sung by William A. Owens.

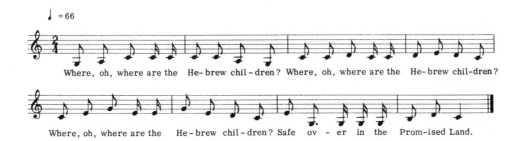

Where, oh, where are the Hebrew children?
Where, oh, where are the Hebrew children?
Where, oh, where are the Hebrew children?
Safe over in the Promised Land.

Where, oh, where is the prophet Daniel?
Etc.

Where, oh, where is my dear mother?
Etc.

I WILL ARISE AND GO TO JESUS

Sung by William A. Owens.

Come, you sinners, poor and needy,
Weak and wounded, sick and sore;
Jesus ready stands to save you,
Full of pity, love and pow'r.

I will arise and go to Jesus;
He will embrace me in his arms,
In the arms of my dear Savior,
Oh, there are ten thousand charms.

ON CANAAN'S HAPPY SHORE

Sung by William A. Owens.

Oh, brothers will you meet me?
Oh, brothers will you meet me?
Oh, brothers will you meet me
On Canaan's happy shore?

By the grace of God I'll meet you,
By the grace of God I'll meet you,
By the grace of God I'll meet you
On Canaan's happy shore.

Singers substituted father, mother, sister, preacher, mourner, and so on to lengthen the song.

AND AM I BORN TO DIE

Sung by William A. Owens.

And am I born to die,
To lay this body down?
And shall I fear to own his cause,
Or blush to speak his name?

THERE'LL BE NO DARK VALLEY

Sung by William A. Owens.

There'll be no dark valley when Jesus comes,
There'll be no dark valley when Jesus comes,
There'll be no dark valley when Jesus comes
To gather his loved ones home;
To gather his loved ones home,
To gather his loved ones home;
There'll be no dark valley when Jesus comes
To gather his loved ones home.

NO, NEVER ALONE

Sung by William A. Owens.

I heard the voice of the Savior
Telling me still to fight on;
He promised never to leave me,
Never to leave me alone.

Refrain:
No, never alone,
No, never alone,
He promised never to leave me,
Never to leave me alone.

COME, HUMBLE SINNERS

Sung by William A. Owens.

Come, humble sinners in whose breast
A thousand thoughts revolve;
Come, with your fear and sin oppressed
And make this last resolve.
Oh, you must be a lover of the Lord,
Or you cain't go to heaven when you die.

THE WICKED DAUGHTER

Sung by Mrs. Jessie Ann Chennault Smith. There is flexibility in tempo and rhythm.

Young peo-ple who ___ de-light in sin, I'll tell you what ___ has late-ly been;

A la-dy who was young and fair, She died in sin ___ and dark de-spair.

Young people who delight in sin,
I'll tell you what has lately been;
A lady who was young and fair,
She died in sin and dark despair.

She went to parties, both dance and play,
In spite of all her friends could say.
"I'll turn to God when I get old
And then he will receive my soul."

One Friday morning she was taken ill,
Her stubborn heart began to yield.
"Alas, alas, my days are spent,
Too late to God now to repent."

She called her mother to her bed,
Her eyes were rolling in her head.
"When I am dead remember well,
Your wicked daughter screams in hell.

"Earthly father, fare thee well;
My soul is lost and doomed to hell;
Those hellish flames around me roll,
Oh, I'm a lost and ruined soul."

She gnawed her tongue before she died;
She wrung her hands and screamed and cried,
"Oh, must I burn forevermore,
Ten thousand years all o'er and o'er?

"Young people now, both great and small,
Take warning by my warning words,
For if you wait till it's too late,
You may expect this awful fate."

THE ORPHAN GIRL

Sung by Daniel Jeffus, Lovelady, Texas, 1938.

"No— home, no home," said the lit-tle— girl At the door of the prince-ly hall, —

As she tremb-ling stood on the pol-ished steps And— leaned on the mar-ble— wall. —

"No home, no home," said the little girl
At the door of the princely hall,
As she trembling stood on the polished steps
And leaned on the marble wall.

"My father, alas, I never knew,"
And a tear dimmed her eye so bright.
"My mother sleeps in a new-made grave,
'Tis an orphan begs tonight."

Her clothes were thin and her feet were bare,
But the snow had covered her head.
"Oh, give me a home," she feebly said,
"A home and a bit of bread."

The night was dark and the snow fell fast
But the rich man closed his door,
And the proud face frowned as he scornfully said,
"No room, no bread for the poor."

The rich man sleeps on his velvet couch
And dreams of his silver and gold.
The orphan lies in her bed of snow
And murmurs, "So cold, so cold."

The morning dawned and the orphan girl
Still lay at the rich man's door,
But her soul had fled to a home above
Where there's room and bread for the poor.

THE ROMISH LADY

Words and tune from Mrs. Martha Davis Lucas, Sherman, Texas.

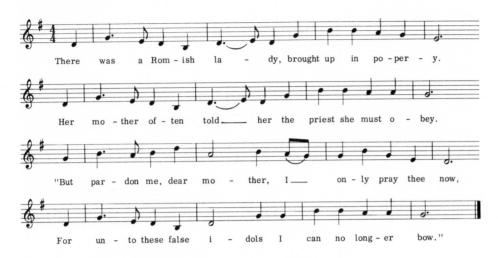

There was a Romish lady, brought up in popery.
Her mother often told her the priest she must obey.
"But pardon me, dear mother, I only pray thee now,
For unto these false idols I can no longer bow."

Assisted by a hand maid a Bible she concealed,
And as she gained instruction the Lord his love revealed;
No longer would she prostrate to pictures made of gold,
And soon she was betrayed and her Bible from her sold.

"I'll bow to my dear Jesus, and worship God unseen;
I'll live by faith forever; the works of man are vain.
I cannot worship idols nor pictures made by man.
Dear mother, use your pleasure, but pardon if you can."

The chains of gold so costly they from this lady took,
And she with all her courage the pride of life forsook.
Before the pope they brought her in hopes of her return,
And there she was condemned in horrid flames to burn.

"It was my cruel mother was on my ruin bent,
'Twas her who did betray me, but I am innocent."
In come her raging mother her daughter to behold,
And in her arms she brought an image decked in gold.

"Oh, take from me those idols, remove them from my sight,
And restore to me my Bible, in it I take delight."
Soon as these words were spoken up stepped the man of death
And kindled up the flames to stop her mortal breath.

"Tormentors, use your pleasure and do as you think best;
I'm in hope my blessed Jesus will take my soul to rest.
With Jesus and his angels I ever hope to dwell;
God pardon priest and people, I bid you all farewell."

AFRO-AMERICAN SPIRITUALS

INTRODUCTION of African slaves into the Jamestown colony in 1619 changed the course of folk music in the South and eventually the course of both folk and art music in all America. In ever increasing numbers slaves were captured on the West Coast of Africa, from among tribes of the Dahomey, Ashanti, Congolese, Mendi, and others. In ever increasing numbers they were sold in America, to be house servants in homes of the rich North and South, to be workers in the tobacco fields or on cotton plantations in the South. By accident or by plan the slaves were so widely dispersed that only rarely would two from the same tribe belong to the same master. They were forced to learn English; tribal languages were, except in a few instances, quickly forgotten.

Tribal cultures also suffered from this dispersion. Without written languages, the Africans had depended on oral tradition for recording and passing on their tribal history and culture, a tradition for which the old were responsible. Slavers bought the young, children even, but rejected the old. In the first generation in America, with no one to recount them, tribal history and law and lore were reduced to remnants, and by the second they were almost entirely forgotten. Their own culture lost, the slaves began assimilating the alien, often with the help of their owners. As the years passed there was a gradual blending of Anglo-Saxon and African until a distinct Afro-American culture was discernible, especially in music.

Whatever else they had lost, Afro-Americans did not lose their distinct sense of sound and rhythm. Probably their first singing of songs of Anglo-Saxon origin was imbued with these. At least some of this singing was in Anglican churches in Virginia. Those plantation owners who were motivated by a genuine missionary feeling taught their slaves the liturgy in their cabins at night and ordered them to sit on the slave benches in Sunday morning services. In the services the slaves were exposed to the stern discipline of English plainsong and the religious fervor of

170

hymns by Isaac Watts and others. As new frontiers opened up, as settlers moved across the Blue Ridge and then the Alleghenies, slaves were admitted to church membership with the whites. The Anglican liturgy left behind, the slaves were taught the hymns both of dissent and of evangelism, and they took quickly to the teaching. Preachers and congregations alike noted the beauty and feeling of their singing, the harmony unlike anything they had heard, the rhythm reminiscent of the beat of the drum.

Early in the nineteenth century slaves had increased in numbers to such an extent that they were able to maintain their own churches. Congregations were segregated; spiritual singing became almost as segregated. At about the same time white churches adopted printed hymnals and their hymn-making became partially circumscribed by the printed page. Slave congregations, unable to read or write, with no books to restrain them, sang the old songs as they remembered them, changed them to their needs, or made up their own songs to record their own experience. Set apart from the whites, the blacks gave way more freely to their own sense of sound and rhythm, and the Negro spiritual became a distinctive contribution to American folk music.

Makers of white spirituals had borrowed tunes and occasionally words from ballads and other secular songs. Makers of black spirituals practiced the same borrowing. Whites sang of the fear of hell, the hope of heaven, and at times let their words be tainted with propaganda against one orthodoxy or another. Blacks also sang of the fear of death, and hope of heaven, and subtly expressed their hatred of bondage, less subtly their hope for freedom. The borrowings of white from black, black from white have been clearly set forth by George Pullen Jackson in his *White and Negro Spirituals: Their Life Span and Kinship.*

The Negro spirituals included here as examples of a distinctive form of folk music were selected from those learned from a lifetime of listening and from over a hundred recordings made in churches and homes in the Brazos River bottoms and in other parts of Texas.

I'VE BEEN LISTENIN' ALL DAY LONG

Sung by the Old Elam Baptist Church congregation, Hearne, Texas, 1938.

The chords are from the piano accompaniment.

Refrain:
> I've been listenin' all day long,
> Been listenin' all night long,
> Been listenin' all day long
> To hear some sinnuh pray.

I know I've been converted
And I ain't gonna make no 'larm;
My soul is anchored in Jesus

And the world cain't do me no harm.
> *(Refrain)*

Some say that John the Baptist
Was nothin' but a Jew,
But the Holy Bible tells us
That John was a preachuh too.
> *(Refrain)*

TRAVELIN' SHOES

Sung by two unidentified boys at St. Philip's College, San Antonio, Texas, 1941.

I saw ol' death come knocking at the sinnuh man's do',
I heard death say, "Come on, sinnuh, ain't you ready to go?"
An' then the sinnuh man he began to cry
An' the water's a-risin' up-a a ankle high;
An' I heard him say, "Lawd, I jes' wants to be."
An' the water's a-risin' up-a around his knee.
An'-a ol' death a-grabbed him an' took him in,
An' the water's a-risin' up-a around his chin,
Sayin' "No, my Lawdy, don't want to go,
'Cause I ain't got no duty,
Ain't got no travelin' shoes."

Oh, I saw ol' death come knocking at my mother's do',
I heard death say, "Come on, mother, ain't you ready to go?"
An' my mother stoop-a down jes' to button up her shoes,
An' she shouted, "Hallelujah, Law'," began to move.
An' she moved on down by the Jurdon's stream,
An' she shouted, "Hallelujah, Lawd, done been redeemed,
'Cause I have done my duty, got on my travelin' shoes,
Got on my travelin' shoes,
Got on my travelin' shoes,
Got on my travelin' shoes."

BY AND BY

Sung by Fanny Givens, Kingsville, Texas, 1941.

The pattern of musical repetition is A B A B C B C B. The rhythm of this song is very difficult to express in musical notation because of the extensive, unmeasured ornamentation.

Oh, by and by, oh, by, by and by
I am going to lay down my heavy heavy load.
Oh, by and by, oh, by, by and by
I am going to lay down my heavy heavy load.

Oh, one of these mornings, sometimes I'm so sad.
I am going to lay down my heavy heavy load.
I'm gonna put on my wings and fly;
I am going to lay down my heavy heavy load.

OH, MY LOVIN' BROTHUH

Sung by Fanny Givens, Kingsville, Texas, 1941.

Although there is rhythmic flexibility in this song, there is also a strong sense
of barline, particularly at the beginning of syncopated measures.

Oh, my lovin' brothuh, when the world's on fia-uh,
Don't you want God's bosom to be yo' pillow?
Hide me ovuh in the rocks of ages,
Rocks of ages clif' fo' me.

Oh, my lovin' sistuh, *etc.*

Oh, my lovin' deacon, *etc.*

Oh, my lovin' preachuh, *etc.*

AFRO-AMERICAN SECULAR SONGS

IN FORM, songs in this collection range from ballad to comic to lullabies to blues, forms that with the exception of the blues run parallel to those of the Anglo-American songs. "The Maid Freed from the Gallows" in dialect begins, "Hanguhman, hanguhman, slack on yo' rope" and "Our Goodman" becomes "The Drunkard's Special." Folk hero and work songs appear in "John Henry" and "Stackolee." Black singers often divided their songs into spirituals and "sinful": anything not spiritual was sinful, and spiritual singers often refused to sing any of the other songs. This division proved impossible to maintain as secular versions of such spirituals as "When the Saints Go Marching In" came into being. Blackface minstrels both imitated and parodied Negro songs, whether spiritual or secular. Black singers both contributed to and borrowed from this minstrelsy. Together they spread such comic lines as

> Run, nigger, run, the pateroller'll catch you;
> Run, nigger, run, it's almost day;
> Nigger run, nigger flew,
> Nigger lost his Sunday shoe.

Together they used the Negro comic song as a vehicle to make fun of both white masters and Negro slaves.

White songs, spiritual and secular, made a circular journey from white singing to black singing and back. White women taught black women to quiet babies, black and white, with lullabies, some of them from the Anglo-Saxon. White children grew up and sang these same lullabies, with dialect, rhythm, and tone from the African added.

The blues has made a similar but more spectacular journey. A form belonging

175

to the twentieth century, it is the first American folk music in which the Anglo-American is subdominant, the Afro-American dominant. As the Negro spiritual is an extension of the white, so is the blues song an extension of certain elements of the black, especially those that in sad tones lament the harshness and loneliness of life. The African tone and syncopation belong to both spiritual and blues. But there are differences. A congregation in religious ecstasy may sing "Let me go, let me go, let me go, let me go . . ." twenty times or more—three syllables on two notes—the only change a subtle shifting of rhythm as they build to a crescendo. A lone blues singer may as often repeat "Sweet mama . . ."—three syllables on two notes—as many times. The difference is that the first has the dynamics of the group, the second the expression of one lonesome singer. One rides on religious emotion, the other on sexual love. A few black spirituals have made their way into white hymnbooks. Blues songs have echoed deep in the white consciousness, whether in the humor of a line like "Every goodbye ain't gone, every shut eye sho' ain't sleep . . ." or in the plaint:

> Oh, T for Texas, T for Tennessee;
> Oh, T for Texas, T for Tennessee;
> I mean it's T for teeny mama, the one I want to see.

OH, MOU'NUHS

AS THE THREE VERSIONS included here show, this song moves freely from white to black and back again. The line "Oh, mou'nuhs, you shall be free" is a remnant of revival meetings in which mourners went to the mourners' bench before the altar to confess their sins and pray for the freedom of salvation. The comic elements were apparently added by blackface minstrels. The song is widely known. The version given here without music is more widely sung than the other two, "Oh, Hear That Trumpet Sound" and "You Shall Be Free."

> Says ole nigger preacher a-settin' on a log,
> Oh, mou'nuhs,
> Finger on the trigger and the sight on the hog,
> Oh, mou'nuhs,
> Says the gun said boom and the hog said zip,
> Says the nigger grabbed that hog with all his grip.
> Oh, mou'nuhs, you shall be free, free,
> Oh, mou'nuhs, you shall be free, free,
> When the good Lord sets you free.
>
> Come around the chicken house on my knees,
> Oh, mou'nuhs,
> Thought I heard a chicken sneeze,

Oh, mou'nuhs,
Sneezed so hard with the whooping cough,
Oh, mou'nuhs,
Like to sneezed his head and his tail right off.
Oh, mou'nuhs, you shall be free, free,
Oh, mou'nuhs, you shall be free, free,
When the good Lord sets you free.

OH, HEAR THAT TRUMPET SOUND

Sung by Rod Drake, Silsbee, Texas, 1952.

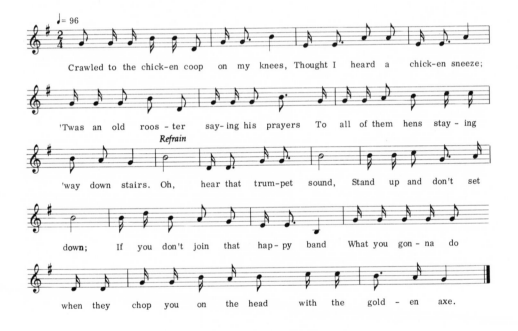

Crawled to the chicken coop on my knees,
Thought I heard a chicken sneeze;
'Twas an old rooster saying his prayers
To all of them hens staying 'way down stairs.

Refrain:
    Oh, hear that trumpet sound,
    Stand up and don't set down;
    If you don't join that happy band
    What you gonna do when they chop you on the head
      with the golden axe.

Well, the hawk's a-setting on the railroad track,
Picking his teeth with a carpet tack,
When he got through he forgot to look around
And I hit him on the head with the golden axe.
        (Refrain)

YOU SHALL BE FREE

Sung by the White sisters, St. Philip's College, San Antonio, Texas, 1941.

I love my wife, I love my baby,
I love my flapjacks a-floatin' in gravy;
I press my dices to make my passes,
I love my flapjacks a-floatin' in 'lasses.
Oh, flapjacks, you shall be free,
In glory, you shall be free,
When the good Lawd sets you free.

Now when I die, don't bury me a-tall,
Hang me high up on the wall;
Grease my heels with tallow and lard,
Throw me right over in some black gal's yard.
In glory, you shall be free,
In glory, you shall be free,
When the good Lawd sets you free.

A big black nigger, black as tar,
Trying to get to heaven on a 'lectric car;
His eyes was red, his gums was blue,

Godamighty struck him and his coattails flew.
Run, nigger man, you shall be free,
In glory, you shall be free,
When the good Lawd sets you free.

Our Father, who art in heaven,
White man owed me twenty dollars, only paid me 'leven;
Kingdom come, Thy will be done,
If I hadn't a-took the 'leven, I wouldn't a got none.
That's a white man, you shall be free,
In glory, you shall be free,
When the good Lawd sets you free.

GO TO SLEEP, LITTLE BABY

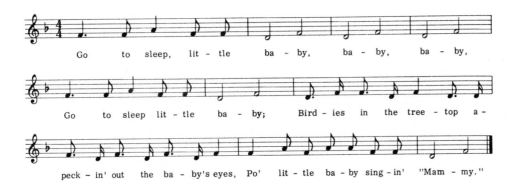

Go to sleep, little baby, baby, baby,
Go to sleep little baby;
Birdies in the treetop a-peckin' out the baby's eyes,
Po' little baby singin' "Mammy."

WELL, THE DAY I LEFT MY PO' MAMA'S DOOR

Sung by Rod Drake, Silsbee, Texas, 1952.

Well, the day I left my po' mama's door,
That's the day that I left my friend,
But the day I takened up with this po' woman wife of mine,
That's the day that my troubles begin.

Refrain:
      Well, a Law' me, Law' po' gal,
      Please to let my troubles go by,
      For I'm in trouble and I'm in trouble deep,
      And if trouble don't kill me I'll live till I die.

Well, if I'd had the wisdom to listen to what my po' mama said,
I'd been now a-sleeping in my po' mama's bed,
But being so young and so foolish, oh, God,
I've given my own self away.
      (*Refrain*)

It was late at night when my po' papa come home,
Said I heard a mighty rapping on my door.
Says, "Who's that rapping on my door?
Please, sir, don't you rap no more."
      (*Refrain*)

Well, hand me down my old valise,
Give me my dirty old clo'se,
And if my mama asks you about me
Tell her that I'm sleeping out o' doors.
(*Refrain*)

GO TO SLEEPY

Go to sleepy little baby,
'Fore the boogerman catch you;
When you wake, gonna have a piece of cake,
A coach and four little ponies:
A dapple and a grey,
And a black and a bay.
Go to sleepy, little baby.

SOURCE NOTES

DURING THE YEARS 1883-1898, Francis James Child published *English and Scottish Popular Ballads*, a five-volume work that included 305 traditional ballads. Since then numerous collections have been published of British folk songs as they have been found in America. Most notable of these is *English Folk Songs from the Southern Appalachians*, collected by Cecil J. Sharp and published in 1932. It is in two volumes and includes 74 ballads and songs. In *The Traditional Tunes and Texts of the Child Ballads*, published in four volumes in 1959-1972, Bertrand Harris Bronson collected all the tunes that he could find in printed or manuscript collections that were associated with the Child texts. For references to these ballads in the following notes there are two numbers separated by a solidus. The first is the number in the Child collection, the second the number in the Bronson collection. An asterisk appearing after the reference indicates that errors in transcription of music and/or text have been corrected. Several ballads have been added which were unknown to Bronson. For these, bibliographical citation consists solely of the Child number.

No comparable work has been done on the Anglo-American ballads and songs not included in Child. Sharp's collection, as the most comprehensive, is cited where appropriate. Other collections are cited for ballads not appearing in Bronson or Sharp, or for significant information. Those used frequently, and therefore with abbreviated references in the notes, include H. M. Belden, *Ballads and Songs Collected by the Missouri Folk-Lore Society* (Columbia, Missouri, 1940); Paul G. Brewster, *Ballads and Songs of Indiana* (Bloomington, Indiana, 1940); John Harrington Cox, *Folk-Songs of the South* (Cambridge, 1925); *Journal of American Folk-Lore*; Louise Pound, *American Ballads and Songs* (New York, 1922); Vance Randolph, *Ozark Folksongs*, 4 vols. (Columbia, Missouri, 1946-48); and Carl Sandburg, *The American Songbag* (New York, 1927).

Titles of songs for which bibliographical information was not readily available have been omitted from the notes.

BRITISH POPULAR BALLADS

ROSEMARY ONE TIME (THE ELFIN KNIGHT). Child 2
PRETTY POLLY (LADY ISABEL AND THE ELF KNIGHT). (a) Child 4; (b) Bronson 4/76
BILLY BOY. Bronson 12, Appendix
HOW COME THAT BLOOD ON YOUR SHIRT SLEEVE (EDWARD). (a) Child 13/4; (b)
    Child 13/21*
THREE BLACK CROWS. Child 26/6*
LOVING HENRY (YOUNG HUNTING). Child 68/3
FAIR ELLENDER (LORD THOMAS AND FAIR ELEANOR). Child 73/10
WHO WILL SHOE YOUR PRETTY LITTLE FOOT (THE LASS OF LOCH ROYAL). (a)
    Child 76/15; (b) Child 76
THE THREE LITTLE BABES (THE WIFE OF USHER'S WELL). Child 79/16*
BARBARA ALLEN. (a) Child 84/67; (b) Child 84
THE HANGMAN'S ROPE (THE MAID FREED FROM THE GALLOWS). Child 95/7
THE FOUR MARYS (MARY HAMILTON). Child 173/9
GYPSY DAVY (THE GYPSY LADDIE). Child 200/124*
THE HOUSE CARPENTER (THE DAEMON LOVER). Child 243/102*
THE DRUNKARD'S SONG (OUR GOODMAN). Child 274/17
TI RISSLETY ROSSLETY (THE WIFE WRAPT IN WETHER'S SKIN). (a) Child 277/61;
    (b) Child 277/62*
THE DEVIL'S SONG (THE FARMER'S FIRST WIFE). Child 278/3*
THE MERRY GOLDEN TREE (THE SWEET TRINITY). Child 286
A RICH IRISH LADY (THE BROWN GIRL). Child 295/45*

ANGLO-AMERICAN BALLADS

WILLIAM HALL, OR THE BRISKY YOUNG FARMER. (a) Sharp 171; (b) Sharp 171
A PRETTY FAIR MAID (a) Sharp 98; (b) Sharp 98
LATE ONE SUNDAY EVENING. Sharp 48
LOVELY WILLIAM. For another fragment see Randolph 113
ONCE I COURTED A FAIR BEAUTY BRIDE. Sharp 110
COME ALL YOU PRETTY FAIR MAIDS. Cecil J. Sharp, *Folk-Songs from Somerset* 1
THE LITTLE SPARROW. Sharp 118
I WAS OUT WALKING. Sharp 145
YOUNG JOHNNIE. (a) Sharp 58; (b) Sharp 58
THE OXFORD GIRL. Sharp 71
THE DRUMMER BOY OF WATERLOO. Cox 82
YOUNG CHARLOTTIE. Brewster 30
THE BUTCHER'S BOY. Sharp 101
THE WILD MOOR. Brewster 45; Cox 148
LITTLE MOHEA. Cox 116; Belden, p. 143
THE JEALOUS LOVER. Cox 38; Brewster 46
THE BANKS OF CLODDIE. Cox 94; Pound 30
FAIR FANNIE MOORE. Cox 94; Pound 30
BROTHER GREEN. Brewster 74; Cox 72
I WAS STANDING ON PICKETS. Sharp 113

JESSE JAMES. Cox 44; Belden, p. 397

THE BOSTON BURGLAR. Pound 23; Brewster 41; Cox 84

TWO ORPHANS. Broadside by P. J. Downey, New York Public Library Collection

THE ROVING GAMBLER. Belden, p. 374

ANGLO-AMERICAN LOVE SONGS

THE SAILOR BOY. Sharp 85

NORA DARLING. Wolford, *The Play-Party in Indiana*, p. 75

THE IRISH GIRL. Sharp 180

FOND AFFECTION. Sharp 111

BURY ME BENEATH THE WILLOW. Belden, p. 482

THE BIRMINGHAM JAIL. Sandburg, p. 148; Lomax, *American Ballads and Folk Songs*,
    p. 147

MY BLUE-EYED BOY. Bronson 76, D11, gives the refrain as a variant of "The Lass of
    Loch Royal"

THEY SAY IT IS SINFUL TO FLIRT. *Journal* 42:278; 45:89

TOO LATE. Spaeth, *Weep Some More, My Lady*, p. 33

ON TOP OF OLD SMOKY. Sharp 117

THE BRIGHT SHERMAN VALLEY. Sandburg, p. 130

GOODBYE, LITTLE BONNIE BLUE EYES. Lunsford and Stringfield, *Thirty and One Folk-
    Songs from the Southern Mountains*, p. 16; Lomax, *Our Singing Country*, p. 148

JACK AND JOE. Neely, *Tales and Songs of Southern Illinois*, p. 244

ANGLO-AMERICAN COMIC SONGS

NODDINGHAM TOWN. Sharp 191

DEAR JOHN. Sharp 132

BRYNIE O'LINN. Sharp 151

JENNIE JENKINS. Sharp 260

THERE WAS AN OLD MAN THAT LIVED ON THE HILL. Sharp 188

DEVILISH MARY. Sharp 149

ROLLY TROODUM. Sharp 128

I WISH I WAS A SINGLE GIRL AGAIN. Sharp 86

THE BLUE-TAILED FLY. Published as a penny song sheet in Baltimore in 1846

THE LAZY MAN. Sharp 182

HURRAH FOR ARKANSAS. Sharp 170

POMPEY SMASH AND DAVY CROCKETT. J. Frank Dobie, ed., *Texas and Southwestern
    Lore* (Publications of the Texas Folklore Society, 6), p. 205

SONGS AND GAMES FOR CHILDREN

COME ALL YOU JOLLY HUNTERS. Sharp 214

FROG WENT A-COURTING. Sharp 220

WAY DOWN SOUTH WHERE I WAS BORN. Sharp 221

WHEN I'SE A LITTLE BOY. Sharp 217

PRETTIEST LITTLE TREE. Sharp 206

HUNTING THE WREN. *Texas and Southwestern Lore*, p. 69; Smith 16
SAW AN OLD CROW. Sharp 222
THE BROWN DUCK. Sharp 226

PLAY-PARTY SONGS AND GAMES

With the exception of "Shoot the Buffalo" and "I'm on My Way to Georgy," sung by Rod Drake, and the version of "Old Joe Clark" sung by Maidy Kelly, the texts and music for these songs were published in *Swing and Turn: Texas Play-Party Games* by William A. Owens (Dallas, 1936).

ANGLO-AMERICAN SPIRITUALS

THE HEBREW CHILDREN. George Pullen Jackson, *White and Negro Spirituals* (New York, 1943), p. 202
I WILL ARISE AND GO TO JESUS. Words by Joseph Hart set to a Southern folk melody. Jackson, *White and Negro Spirituals,* p. 204; *Baptist Hymnal* (Nashville, 1956)
AND AM I BORN TO DIE. Jackson, *White and Negro Spirituals*, p. 169
COME, HUMBLE SINNERS. Jackson, *White and Negro Spirituals,* p. 146; words attributed to Isaac Watts
THE WICKED DAUGHTER. George Pullen Jackson, *White Spirituals in the Southern Uplands* (Chapel Hill, 1933), p. 191
THE ROMISH LADY. Jackson, *White Spirituals*, p. 188

AFRO-AMERICAN SPIRITUALS

TRAVELIN' SHOES, a fragment in John Lovell, Jr., *Black Song* (New York, 1972), p. 208

AFRO-AMERICAN SECULAR SONGS

OH, MOU'NUHS. Newman I. White, *American Negro Folk-Songs* (Hatboro, Pennsylvania, 1965), p. 192
GO TO SLEEPY. *Journal* 44:419

INDEX OF TITLES

INDEX OF FIRST LINES